DISABILITY AND THE DISABLED - ISSUES, LAWS AND PROGRAMS

CAN WE PREDICT MATHEMATICAL DISABILITIES FROM ABILITIES IN KINDERGARTEN?

DISABILITY AND THE DISABLED - ISSUES, LAWS AND PROGRAMS

Additional books in this series can be found on Nova's website under the Series tab.

Additional E-books in this series can be found on Nova's website under the E-book tab.

DISABILITY AND THE DISABLED - ISSUES, LAWS AND PROGRAMS

CAN WE PREDICT MATHEMATICAL DISABILITIES FROM ABILITIES IN KINDERGARTEN?

ANNEMIE DESOETE
AND
PIETER STOCK

Nova Science Publishers, Inc.
New York

Copyright © 2011 by Nova Science Publishers, Inc.

All rights reserved. No part of this book may be reproduced, stored in a retrieval system or transmitted in any form or by any means: electronic, electrostatic, magnetic, tape, mechanical photocopying, recording or otherwise without the written permission of the Publisher.

For permission to use material from this book please contact us:
Telephone 631-231-7269; Fax 631-231-8175
Web Site: http://www.novapublishers.com

NOTICE TO THE READER

The Publisher has taken reasonable care in the preparation of this book, but makes no expressed or implied warranty of any kind and assumes no responsibility for any errors or omissions. No liability is assumed for incidental or consequential damages in connection with or arising out of information contained in this book. The Publisher shall not be liable for any special, consequential, or exemplary damages resulting, in whole or in part, from the readers' use of, or reliance upon, this material.

Independent verification should be sought for any data, advice or recommendations contained in this book. In addition, no responsibility is assumed by the publisher for any injury and/or damage to persons or property arising from any methods, products, instructions, ideas or otherwise contained in this publication.

This publication is designed to provide accurate and authoritative information with regard to the subject matter covered herein. It is sold with the clear understanding that the Publisher is not engaged in rendering legal or any other professional services. If legal or any other expert assistance is required, the services of a competent person should be sought. FROM A DECLARATION OF PARTICIPANTS JOINTLY ADOPTED BY A COMMITTEE OF THE AMERICAN BAR ASSOCIATION AND A COMMITTEE OF PUBLISHERS.

Full color presentation of graphics is available in the E-book.

LIBRARY OF CONGRESS CATALOGING-IN-PUBLICATION DATA

Desoete, Annemie.
 Can we predict mathematical disabilities from abilities in kindergarten /
Annemie Desoete and Pieter Stock.
   p. cm.
 Includes index.
 ISBN 978-1-61668-762-5 (softcover)
 1. Mathematics--Study and teaching (Early childhood) 2. Mathematical
ability--Testing. 3. Learning disabilities--Diagnosis. 4. Early childhood
education. I. Stock, Pieter. II. Title.
 QA135.6.D484 2009
 372.7--dc22
                        2010025393

Published by Nova Science Publishers, Inc. † *New York*

CONTENTS

Preface		**vii**
Chapter 1	Introduction	**1**
Chapter 2	Pilot Study on Early Markers for Mathematical Difficulties	**17**
Chapter 3	Screening for Mathematical Disabilities in Kindergarten: A Cross-sectional Study	**23**
Chapter 4	Mastery of Counting Principles in Toddlers: A Longitudinal Study	**29**
Chapter 5	Detecting Children with Disabilities in Kindergarten? Longitudinal Study 4	**35**
Chapter 6	Study 5	**41**
Chapter 7	General Discussion	**47**
References		**73**
Index		**93**

PREFACE

Preparatory abilities acquired in kindergarten are found to be strong predictors for later arithmetic proficiency. A research investigation was designed to examine if the level of children's mathematical abilities in first and second grade could be predicted from their performance on preparatory abilities in kindergarten. For this purpose children were followed from kindergarten to second grade. The results indicate that good predictions of beginning mathematical abilities can be made. Even long term predictions are possible of later mathematical performances, especially for the domain of mental arithmetics and number knowledge. It is advised to assess a set of preparative arithmetic abilities including logic thinking abilities and counting knowledge in kindergarten.

We first will discuss the theoretical background of the study. Further, the main findings of the pilot study and the four studies on logical abilities, counting abilities and magnitude comparison as important preparatory arithmetic abilities will be addressed. Next, we will focus on the conclusions of all studies and on the implications of the use of different selection criteria in order to define children with mathematical disabilities.

Chapter 1

INTRODUCTION

Here we discuss the theoretical background of this study. We focus on mathematical disabilities and give an overview of the main abilities that have been indicated as possible markers for the development of arithmetic disabilities. Furthermore, we formulate the objectives and research questions of the five studies in this research investigation.

1.1. Mathematical Disabilities[1]

Recent research findings demonstrate that between 3 and 14 percent of school-age children have some form of arithmetic disability (Barbaresi, Katusic, Colligan, Waever, & Jacobsen, 2005; Desoete, 2007a, 2008a; 2010; Desoete & Veenman, 2006a, 2006b; Dowker, 2005; Geary, 2004; Shalev, Manor, & Gross-Tsur, 2005). These figures were confirmed by several researchers in different countries (Badian, 1983; Desoete, Roeyers, & De Clercq, 2004; Gross-Tsur, Manor, & Shalev, 1996; Klauer, 1992; Kosc, 1974; Lewis, Hitch, & Walker, 1994; von Aster, Deloche, Dellatolas, & Meier, 1997). Similar prevalence rates have been found in

---

[1] This section is based on Stock (2008) and on Desoete (2007a) as well as on Stock, P., Desoete, A. & Roeyers, H. (2006). Focussing on mathematical disabilities: a search for definition, classification and assessment (pp. 29-62). In Soren V. Randall (Ed.) Learning Disabilities New Research Nova Science: Hauppauge, NY

boys and girls (Lewis et al., 1994), with boys doing slightly better (Gross-Tsur et al., 1996 (1:1.1), Klauer, 1992, von Aster, 2000).

With the high prevalence of arithmetic disabilities, comes a proliferation of terms used in the description of the disabilities (Desoete et al., 2004; Desoete, 2008a, 2008b; 2010; Kavale & Forness, 2000): *dyscalculia* (Njiokikitjien, 2004; von Aster et al., 1997), *developmental dyscalculia* (Shalev, Auerbach, Manor, & Gross-Tsur, 2000; Kosc, 1974; Gross-Tsur et al., 1996), *mathematical disabilities* (Kulak, 1993; Light & DeFries, 1995), *arithmetic disabilities* (Badian, 1983), *arithmetic disorders* (Lewis et al., 1994) or even *acalculia* (Denburg & Tranel, 2003). In this book we consistently chose to use the term *arithmetic disabilities*. Commonly, the terms *mathematical or arithmetic difficulties* (Dowker, 2004) and *mathematical or arithmetic problems* are used when arithmetic skills are weak, but are not within the clinical range.

Three important criteria in defining arithmetic disabilities can be distinguished: the retardiation criterion, the resistance criterion (or 'RTI' meaning lack of Response to Instruction) and the exclusion criterion (Geary, 2004; Mazzocco & Myers, 2003; Murphy, Mazzocco, Hanich, & Early, 2007; Ofiesch, 2006; Shalev et al., 2000; Stock, Desoete, & Roeyers, 2009a).

The main criterion that is currently used, is the *retardation criterion* (Geary, 2004). This criterion stipulates that a diagnosis of an arithmetic disability is only justified when a great retardation or below average performance on arithmetic achievement is seen (Desoete et al., 2010; Stock et al., 2006). This criterion is often used in legislative classifications as a prerequisite for refund of treatment and is also found in international classification systems like the ICD-10 (WHO, 1992) and the Diagnostic and statistical manual of mental disorders (DSM-IV; APA, 2000). Although the retardation criterion is used in research and clinical practice, the criterion is unclear because a much variation exists in its interpretation (Geary, Hoard, Byrd-Craven, Nugent, & Numtee, 2007; Kavale & Forness, 2000). In line with the recent research of Murphy and colleagues (2007), the classification of children with arithmetic disabilities when they successively had scores less than the 11th percentile for two or more years

Introduction   3

is defended. Children should also be classified as having arithmetic problems[2] when they perform between the 11th and 25th percentile for two or more years. We further elaborate on the choice of a cut-off for the retardation criterion.

The third and last criterion in defining arithmetic disabilities is the *exclusion criterion*. This criterion states that the disability in arithmetic development can not be explained by handicapping conditions in the situation of the child (e.g., sensory impairments, mental retardation or impairments in general intelligence, social or emotional disturbances, etc.) and external factors (e.g., insufficient or inappropriate instruction, cultural differences, psychogenic factors, etc.) (APA, 2000; WHO, 1992).

These criteria make it possible to give a descriptive diagnosis of mathematical disabilities. There are several theories that partially explain the development of mathematical disabilities, but no single theory can give a full understanding of these disabilities currently (Shalev & Gross-Tsur, 2001). Although it is not yet possible to give an explanatory diagnosis, it is clear that the aetiology of the disorder is multifactorial, including both genetic and environmental factors (Haskell, 2000; Light & DeFries, 1995; Shalev, 2004). It was found that the risk for developing arithmetic disabilities was ten times higher for family members of children with a diagnosis (Shalev et al., 2001). Although a lot of neuroimaging studies have been performed, there is not yet a clear explanation on the neuroanatomic basis of arithmetic, but frontal, precentral, and dorsal parietal areas seem to play an important role (Shalev, 2004). Furthermore, the biological basis of arithmetic can be influenced by contextual factors like instruction, curriculum, and social support (Haskell, 2000; Reusser, 2000). Some authors do not label these problems as arithmetic disabilities but rather as arithmetic difficulties when contextual factors have a major contribution (Mazzocco, 2005).

Doing mathematics is a complex neuropsychological operation involving many basic mathematical abilities (Cornoldi & Lucangeli, 2004; Shalev & Gross-Tsur, 2001). Many authors have tried to build theoretical

---

[2] Across this study, these children are also labelled as low achieving in mathematics or as children with subclinical scores on arithmetic tests.

models of mathematical (dis)functioning. Some models focus on immature counting and calculation strategies (Geary, 2004; Jordan, Hanich, & Kaplan, 2003), slow serial elaboration (Geary & Brown, 1991), deficits in the working memory or speed of processing (Geary, Hoard, Byrd-Craven, & Nugent, 2007; Ketelsen & Welsh, 2010), problems retrieving from semantic long term memory (Geary, 2004), problems with visual spatial elaboration (Geary, 2004; Shalev, 2004), and executive deficits (Passolunghi & Siegel, 2004). McCloskey and colleagues (McCloskey, Caramazza, & Basili, 1985; McCloskey & Macaruso, 1995) proposed a neurocognitive model of mathematical abilities with three numerical components: number comprehension, number production, and comprehension and application of mathematical concepts. Dehaene et al. (Dehaene, 1992; Dehaene & Cohen, 1991; Dehaene, Spelke, Pinel, Stanescu, & Tsivkin, 1999; Dehaene et al., 1996) proposed a triple code model based on a verbal and visuospatial network comprised of verbal, visual, and quantity representations. This model was criticized by Campbell and Clark (1988), and as a reaction they formulated an encoding complex theory. Besides these models, different research findings have discerned other neurologic and neurocognitive structures that are important in mathematics (Burbaud et al., 1995; Rickard et al., 2000; Stanescu-Cosson et al., 2000; Van Harskamp & Cipolotti, 2001). Despite the existence of all these theoretical models there is not yet a unifying model that can provide clear explanations for the development of mathematical (dis)abilities.

Inclusion of a broad variety of involved abilities in doing mathematics leads to a large spectrum of mathematical disabilities based on the failure in one or several distinct basic mathematical abilities. Many researchers have attempted to make a classifications of different combinations and have described several subtypes of mathematical disabilities (Fuchs & Fuchs, 2002; Knopik, Alarcón, & Defries, 1997; Korhonen, 1991; Kronenberger & Dunn, 2003; Padget, 1998; Stock at al., 2006). In general, four subtypes of mathematical disabilities have been described based on procedural deficits, semantic memory deficits, visuospatial deficits, and number knowledge deficits.

Introduction 5

The first subtype concerns a pattern of impairment in mathematical procedures (Cornoldi & Lucangeli, 2004; Geary, 2004; Hécaen, Angelergues, & Huillier, 1961; Kosc, 1974; von Aster, 2000). Children (or adults) with this type of mathematical disability make mistakes in the use of mathematical procedures and have difficulties in keeping track of the order of different steps in complex calculations. The second subtype is described as a semantic memory subtype (Cornoldi & Lucangeli, 2004; Fisk & Rourke, 1979; Geary, 2004; Njiokiktjien, 2004; Rourke, 1989, 1993, 1995; Rourke & Conway, 1997; Rourke & Finlayson, 1978; Rourke & Fuerst, 1995; Strang & Rourke, 1983; von Aster, 2000). Generally, arithmetic facts are not automatized, therefore simple mathematical problems have to be calculated. The third subtype is characterized by problems with insight in and notions of space and is described as visuospatial disabilities in the mathematical domain (Badian, 1983; Fisk & Rourke, 1979; Hécaen et al., 1961; Njiokiktjien, 2004; Rourke, 1989, 1993, 1995; Rourke & Conway, 1997; Rourke & Finlayson, 1978; Rourke & Fuerst, 1995; Shalev, 2004; Strang & Rourke, 1983; von Aster, 2000). The fourth and last described subtype in mathematical disabilities concerns number knowledge deficits (Cornoldi & Lucangeli, 2004; Hécaen et al., 1961; Kosc, 1974; Njiokiktjien, 2004; von Aster, 2000) . People with this sort of mathematical disability lack insight of the structure of the number system and do not know the specific positions for units, tens, and hundreds.

There is scientific evidence for at least the first two subtypes (Desoete et al., 2010; Geary, 1993; 2004; Robinson et al., 2002; Rouselle & Noël, 2007; Temple, 1999). The procedural subtype would be due to executive dysfunction and characterized by a developmental delay in the acquisition of counting and counting procedures used to solve simple arithmetic problems. The semantic subtype would be due to verbal memory dysfunction and characterized by errors in the retrieval of arithmetic facts (Wilson, Revkin, Cohen D., Cohen L., & Dehaene, 2006). However, the borders between different subtypes are vague and the different forms can not be explained separately (Njiokikitjien, 2004). The functioning of one mathematical ability will influence the functioning and development of other mathematical abilities. Furthermore, since mathematical disabilities are a developmental disorder, manifestations of the disability are relative to age and developmental processes (Shalev & Gross-Tsur, 2001).

The manifestation of mathematical disabilities is different in every child, thwarting the diagnostic process. In their research on diagnostic criteria, Mazzocco and Myers (2003) concluded that the number of children with mathematical disabilities varied in function to the definition for mathematical disabilities and/or the diagnostic tool they used. Besides the need for a consensus in defining mathematical disabilities, these findings implicate that clinicians and researchers have to be careful in selecting an appropriate assessment since different assessment tools lead to different clinical classifications (Grégoire & Desoete, 2009).

Nowadays, there are many diagnostic tools designed to diagnose mathematical disabilities (see also Denburg & Tranel, 2003; Mazzocco & Myers, 2003; Njiokikitjien, 2004; Shalev, 2004; Shalev & Gros-Tsur, 2001; von Aster, 2000). Mainstream tests address theassessment of performance of specific mathematical abilities. In Belgium for instance, practitioners often use the Revised Kortrijk Arithmetic test (Kortrijkse Rekentest Revision, KRT-R; Baudonck et al., 2006) and the Arithmetic Number Facts Test (Tempo Test Rekenen, TTR; de Vos, 1992). Although it was found that the use of a single performance-based test was not reliable for the detection of children with mathematical disabilities (Desoete et al., 2004), the use of these kind of tests still remains popular in clinical practice. Only the combination of several diagnostic instruments could prevent the conclusion that the diagnosis was determined by the choice of test (Desoete et al., 2004; Kamphaus, Petosky, & Rowe, 2000; Mazzocco & Myers, 2003). Furthermore, the diagnosis of mathematical disabilities can only be drawn from a broad assessment of the child which including learning, intelligence, and contextual variables. In sum, it is important to distinguish delay and deficit and to consider consistency in performance – both at a point in time and over time. (Hanley, 2005; Mazzocco & Myers, 2003). Since mathematical capacities are dynamic, there is much variability in the developmental process (Shalev, 2004). The individual profile of strengths and weaknesses can shift over time as a function of the growth process. This makes a one-time assessment unreliable (Gersten et al., 2005; Mazzocco & Myers, 2003).

1.2. PREPARATORY MARKERS FOR MATHEMATICAL DISABILITIES

Several cognitive antecedents have been suggested as factors that play a role in the development of initial mathematical performance and eventually as early markers for mathematical difficulties. In 1941, Piaget postulated that logical abilities are conditional to the development of mathematics (Piaget & Szeminska, 1941). However, currently the debate on the value of the Piagetian abilities for mathematics remains unsolved (Lourenço & Machado, 1996). Besides logical abilities, reseachers have focused on the importance of procedural and conceptual counting knowledge in the development of mathematical performance. Finally, since Landerl, Bevan and Butterworth (2004) suggested that the core problem of mathematical disabilities is a magnitude processing deficit, it may be interesting to explore if symbolic or non-symbolic (subitizing) magnitude comparison can be used as early markers for mathematical difficulties (Desoete, Ceulemans, De Weerdt, &Pieters, 2011; Mussolin, Meijas, & Noel, 2010; Piazza et al., 2010). According to the 'defective number module hypothesis' (e.g., Butterworth, 2005) children with mathematical disabilities are expected to have problems with symbolic and non-symbolic tasks. According to the 'access deficit hypothesis' (e.g., Rousselle & Noel, 2007) children with mathematical learning disabilities are supposed to have problems with the symbolice (number-word and Arabic number) tasks but not the the non-symcolic (dot) comparison tasks.

The term 'preparatory abilities' is used here to address the mathematical abilities that already develop in children before they enter formal schooling and learn explicitly to calculate and retrieve arithmetic facts (Desoete & Stock, 2010). With the use of this term we indicate the importance of those precursors without claiming that mastery of these abilities is conditional to a childs mathematical development (Dowker, 2005; Van De Rijt, Van Luit, & Pennings, 1996; Van Luit, 2002).

1.2.1. The Role of Logical Abilities

Some of the best described preparatory mathematical abilities in kindergartners are logical abilities. The definition of these abilities is formulated in Piagets basic work on the numerical development of the child (Piaget & Szeminska, 1941). In this work, "La genèse du nombre chez l'enfant", Piaget postulated from a cognitive point of view that four logical abilities are conditional to the development of mathematics, namely seriation, classification, conservation, and inclusion. The definitions of these concepts are formulated in the following chapter. Piaget (1965) argued that the full development of number comprehension is only possible when the child masters these four logical abilities. Since the publication of the work of Piaget, much criticism of his theories has been formulated (for an overview, see Lourenço & Machado, 1996). Although the work of Piaget remains an essential reference for practitioners working with children with mathematical problems (Grégoire, 2005), the Piagetian logical abilities are no longer considered conditional, but rather as preparatory abilities in mathematical development.

Classification is relevant in knowing the cardinal of a set (e.g., 'How many balls can you see on this picture?'), whereas seriation is needed when dealing with ordinal numbers (e.g., 'Circle the third ball from the beginning.'). Seriation and classification have been found to be basic abilities for in mathematical development (Cornoldi & Lucangeli, 2004). Moreover, seriation tasks in preschool predicted number-line comprehension in first-grade children (Kingma, 1984), whereas classification was not suitable as a predictor of computational skills in grade 1 (Kingma, 1983). The child's acquisition of conservation reflects the ability to think in a reversible way. This way of thinking is especially beneficial for solving reversal addition and subtraction tasks (e.g., '2 + _ =

Introduction 9

5'); significant correlations between number conservation and mathematical performance have been found. Recently it was found that performance on number conservation tasks increased when children were able to count (Dowker, 2005). According to Kingma (1983), the combination of conservation and seriation is a predictor of number-language.

It was found that whether a child has reached the stage of concrete operations or not was an important component of a child's academic readiness (Arlin, 1981). Nunes and colleagues (2006) found that logical abilities and working memory in six year old children predicted mathematical abilities 16 months later. Even after controlling for working memory, logical abilities remained a strong predictor of mathematical abilities. Furthermore, based on an intervention study, they concluded that children who were trained in logical abilities made more progress in mathematical abilities (Nunes et al., 2006). Children who were able to solve logic thinking tasks were found to have better performance on mathematical tests, including items in numerical format and word problems (Grégoire, 2005). These studies supported the hypothesis that there is a strong causal link between logical abilities and mathematical abilities (Nunes et al., 2006), suggesting that logical abilities could be important preparatory markers for the early detection of a deficient in mathematical development.

1.2.2. Counting Knowledge

Besides the Piagetian operations, counting knowledge also seems to be important in the development of mathematics (Baroody, 1992; Frank, 1989; Gersten et al., 2005; Johansson, 2005; Sophian, 1992; Van De Rijt & Van Luit, 1999). Many researchers focused from different theoretical frameworks on the importance of counting knowledge in the development of mathematical abilities (Le Corre, Van de Walle, Brannon, & Carey, 2006; LeFevre et al., 2006). Counting has been described as the key ability that forms the bridge between the innate sense of numerosity and the more advanced mathematical abilities that are culturally expected (Butterworth, 2004). There appears to be a preverbal counting system with which very young children can enumerate or count small sets of objects (up to three or four, Sharon & Wynn, 1998; Starkey, 1992; Wynn, 1996). This early competency later forms the bais for the understanding that serial-ordered words can be used for counting (Geary, 2000).

Children's basic conceptual understanding of how to count objects and their knowledge of the order of numbers play an important role in the development of mathematical abilities. There are two explanations for this prominent role of counting knowledge (Aunola et al., 2004). First, counting leads to the automatic use of math-related information, which enables one to deal with more complex mathematical processes. Secondly, subsequent counting activities lead to the automation of arithmetic facts (Aunola et al., 2004; Van De Rijt & Van Luit, 1999) resulting in more accurate fact retrieval (Aunola et al., 2004) and better mathematical strategies for addition, subtraction (Le Fevre et al., 2006), and multiplication (Blöte, Lieffering, & Ouwehand, 2006). It is obvious that early mathematical strategies for addition and subtraction involves counting in the 'count all' or 'sum' strategy in which the child first counts each collection and then counts the combination of two collections starting from one (e.g., $2 + 5 = \_ 1, 2 \dots 1, 2, 3, 4, 5 \dots 1, 2, 3, 4, 5, 6, 7$). As practice increases, older children use more effective back-up strategies, such as the 'count-on' strategy where they count up from the first addend the number of times indicated by the second addend (e.g., $2 + 5 = \_ (2), 3, 4, 5, 6, 7$) or the 'min' strategy where they count up from the larger addend the number of times indicated by the smaller addend (e.g., $2 + 5 = 5 + 2 = (5), 6, 7$). It is assumed that the retrieval strategy (e.g. '2+5=7, I know this by heart.') is made possible by the learning and progressive strengthening of memory associations between problems and answers as a result of the repeated use of algorithms (Barrouillet & Lepine, 2005; Torbeyns, Verschaffel, & Ghesquière, 2004).

There is a growing body of research on the counting knowledge of children with mathematical disabilities. It is advantageous to use models of normal development of mathematical abilities to study deficient abilities in children with mathematical disabilities (Geary, 2004; Geary, Hamson, & Hoard, 2000). Aunola, Leskinen, Lerkkanen, and Nurmi (2004) followed 194 children from preschool to second grade and found the initial level of counting knowledge in preschool to be the best predictor of later mathematical abilities and amount of growth in mathematical abilities over years. Maturity and efficiency of counting strategies has also been found to be an important predictor of students' ability to profit from mathematical instruction (Gersten et al., 2005). It was further found that children with low performances on addition tasks or problems in retrieving basic arithmetic facts and computing mathematical exercises in first grade had immature counting knowledge (Geary, 1994; Geary, Bow-Thomas, & Yao, 1992; Shalev, 2004). Children who had difficulties in any aspect of counting had weaker performance at standardised mathematical tests, even when compared with children with mathematical difficulties who had no problems with counting knowledge (Dowker, 2001). Furthermore, children who could not sufficiently use their counting knowledge in solving mathematical problems had poor skills in detecting and correcting counting errors (Ohlsson & Rees, 1991). Finally, evidence was found for a different acquisition and development of counting knowlegde in children with mathematical disabilities (Porter, 1998).

Although a lot of research investigated counting as a unitary ability, Dowker (2005) suggested that counting knowledge consists of procedural and conceptual aspects. Procedural and conceptual counting knowledge are strongly related to each other, but they are described as two distinct abilities children have to learn (Le Fevre et al., 2006). It was found that difficulties associated with procedural counting knowledge cannot account for the differences found in conceptual counting knowledge (Sophian, Wood, & Vong, 1995). Procedural counting knowledge is defined as children's ability to perform a mathematical task, for example, when a child can successfully determine that there are five objects in an array (LeFevre et al., 2006). The knowledge of the sequence of counting words (the number row) is one of the most important procedural aspects of counting. This also includes the ability to count forward and backwards easily.

Besides the procedural aspect of counting knowledge, we can discern conceptual counting knowledge. Conceptual knowledge reflects a child's understanding of why a procedure works or whether a procedure is legitimate (LeFevre et al., 2006). The conceptual aspect of counting knowledge contains the mastery of the counting principles. Gelman and Gallistel (1978) described five implicit conceptual principles in counting: the stable order principle, the one-one-correspondence principle, the cardinality principle, the abstraction principle, and the order-irrelevance principle. These principles are further illustrated in chapter two and four, while for an extensive description of the development of the counting principles, we refer to Gallistel and Gelman (1990; Gelman & Gallistel, 1978; Gelman, 1990) and Sophian and Kailihiwa (1998).

Johansson (2005) studied the role of procedural counting knowledge in a group of 126 children in kindergarten and first grade. He concluded that scores on procedural counting knowledge could predict the number and solving strategy of mathematical problems. In their attempt to predict mathematical abilities in second grade based on the abilities in kindergarten, Lepola, et al. (2005) found that only number sequence skills were significant predictors. Even children of nine or ten years sometimes showed difficulties in counting when this involved counting forward and backward from different starting numbers; and such children tended to have other mathematical difficulties (Houssart, 2001). Geary and colleagues (1992) compared typical children and children with mathematical disabilities at the age of six and found that children out of the last group were more likely to make procedural errors in counting. Besides this, they found that some children with mathematical disabilities still showed conceptual difficulties.

Some advocates of the 'continuity hypothesis' (e.g., Gallistel & Gelman, 1992) claimed that children have conceptual knowledge before their procedural counting abilities are well developed. Other researchers reported the opposite (e.g., Frye, Braisby, Lowe, Maroudas, & Nicholls, 1989). The timing of the two types of knowledge may however largely depend on the particular task or the development may be iterative (Rittle-Johnson, Siegler, & Wagner, 2001).

Gelman and Gallistel (1978; Gelman, 1990) argued that there are three innate counting principles that guide children's acquisition of the counting list: the stable order principle, the one-one-correspondence principle, and the cardinality principle. Mastery of these three principles forms the skeletal structure for children's emerging knowledge of counting (Geary, 2004; Gelman & Meck, 1983). The assumption that mastery of these three counting principles is an innate ability is debated heavily, but researchers agreed on the importance of this id (Wynn, 1992). Moreover, mastery of the cardinality principle can be seen as one of the main foundations for a good development of several mathematical abilities (Dowker, 2005). The other two principles, the abstraction principle and the order-irrelevance principle, have been approached as unessential counting principles because violation of these principles does not result in incorrect counting (Briars & Siegler, 1984; Le Fevre et al, 2006).

During the development of counting knowledge, children incorporate both essential and unessential principles in their counting knowledge, but do not continue using the unessential principles over time. Evidence has been found that children with good mathematical abilities progressed faster through this developmental learning process than children who performed worse on mathematical abilities tests (Le Fevre et al., 2006) and that children with mathematical disabilities had difficulties with the unessential features (Geary et al., 1992; Geary et al., 2000; Geary, 2004). In chapter 4 we will further elaborate on the importance of mastery of the counting principles.

1.2.3. Magnitude Comparison

Recently, representation of number size was found to be also involved in numerical competence (Butterworth, 2005; Jordan, Kaplan, Olah, & Locuniak, 2006; Rousselle & Noel, 2007). This numerical skill is involved in subitizing and in magnitude comparison. Subitizing is the rapid apprehension of small numerosity, while magnitude comparison holds that children have to know which number in a pair is larger (Gersten & Chard,

1999; Hannula & Lechtinnen, 2005). Magnitude comparison was found to be an important preparatory predictor of variations in mathematical abilities (Durand, Hulme, Larkin, & Snowling, 2005). Furthermore, there are arguments that problems encountered by children with mathematical disabilities may be due to a deficit in this ability (Butterworth, 2005; Gersten et al., 2005; Holloway & Ansari, 2008; Landerl et al., 2004). Desoete and Grégoire (2007) found that about one third of children with mathematical disabilities had problems with magnitude comparison, though poor performers in first grade had below-average abilities to compare dot sets as preschoolers. Moreover a longitudinal study revealed that children with mathematical disabilities had already deficits in non-symbolic and symbolic Arabic number comparison skills in kindergarten, whereas in grade 2 the deficits in processing symbolic information remained (Desoete et al., 2011).

1.3. Research Focus and Overview of the Studies on Kindergarten Markers

Currently there is much of interest in early detection of children with mathematical disabilities. This interest is stimulated by the fact that if markers can be recognised, it may be possible to prevent children from falling further behind (Gersten et al., 2005; Pasnak, Cooke, & Hendricks, 2006). Early mathematical ability has been found to be the strongest predictor of later school achievement (Duncan et al., 2007), but inconsistent results on the importance of preparatory mathematical abilities are found. Furthermore, few large-scale studies have been done (Porter, 1998). The principal aim of these studies was to investigate the role of preparatory mathematical abilities in the prediction of later mathematical performance in a large group of children with a broad range of mathematical abilities. We focus on seriation, classification, and conservation as important logical abilities, counting knowledge, and magnitude comparison. Making abstractions of other important variables in

Introduction

the development of mathematical (dis)abilities, we investigate if it is possible to detect children with mathematical disabilities based on their performances on preparatory mathematical abilities in kindergarten. Special attention is given to the role of criteria used to define children with mathematical disabilities. Table 1 gives an overview of the studies.

Study 1 served as a pilot study in this research investigation. A rather limited group of 108 children was assessed and we examine if we can predict the level of a child's mathematical ability in first grade based on their performance in kindergarten. It was further tested whether children at-risk for mathematical disabilities in first grade can be detected by their preparatory mathematical abilities in kindergarten.

Based on the promising findings of study 1 a larger sample of children was assessed. Study 2 presents a cross-sectional design with 361 children in kindergarten. Children who arewere low achieving or at least moderately achieving on numerical tests in kindergarten were selected. We focus on differences between these two groups in the performances of preparatory mathematical abilities like counting knowledge, logical abilities, and magnitude comparison. Furthermore, we investigate the role of those abilities in identifying children who are at-risk for developing mathematical disabilities.

The children described in study 2 were further followed in first grade (additional data were added). Since it has been found that counting knowledge is an important preparatory mathematical ability (Baroody, 1992; Frank, 1989; Gersten et al., 2005; Johansson, 2005; Sophian, 1992; Van De Rijt & Van Luit, 1999) and that children with mathematical disabilities differ from typically achieving children in the extent to which they master the essential counting principles (Geary, 2004; Le Fevre et al., 2006), we set up study 3 that focuses on the essential counting principles. Mastery of the stable order, the one-one-correspondence, and the cardinality principle in kindergarten was assessed in a large group of children with a broad range of mathematical abilities ($N = 423$). We examine the frequency of mastery of the essential counting principles in kindergartners. Furthermore, we analyse the relation with mathematical abilities in first grade using multilevel analyses. Study 4 presents a three-year-longitudinal study on 684 children. This study includes two cohorts of children. We examine if it is possible to predict the level of children's mathematical abilities in first and second grade from their performance on preparatory mathematical abilities in kindergarten. Furthermore, the role of intelligence in the assessment of developing mathematical reasoning and numerical facility is investigated. Based on the longitudinal study presented in study 4, children are selected as having mathematical disabilities, as low achieving, or typically achieving in mathematics. In the next study we investigate whether it is possible to find group differences in logical abilities, counting knowledge, and performances on magnitude comparison tasks between children with mathematical disabilities, low achieving, and typically achieving children. The second purpose of this fourth study is to determine if it is possible to detect children with mathematical disabilities based on the preparatory mathematical abilities as measured in kindergarten.

Table 1. Overview of the studies

	Class or period	Research focus
Study 1	kindergarten - 1st grade	Procedural CK, conceptual CK, seriation, classification, conservation, magnitude comparison
Study 2	kindergarten	Procedural CK, conceptual CK, seriation, classification, conservation, magnitude comparison
Study 3	kindergarten - 1st grade	Essential counting principles
Study 4	kindergarten - 2nd grade	Procedural CK, conceptual CK, seriation, classification, conservation, intelligence
Study 5	kindergarten - 2nd grade	Procedural CK, conceptual CK, seriation, classification, magnitude comparison Choice of retardation criterion

Note. Kindergarten = last kindergarten class. CK = counting knowledge.

Finally, the general discussion contains an overview of the main findings. Implications, limitations, and challenges for future research are discussed.

Chapter 2

PILOT STUDY ON EARLY MARKERS FOR MATHEMATICAL DIFFICULTIES[1]

2.1. METHOD

2.1.1. Aim and Research Questions

Study 1 was designed as a pilot study to examine if we can predict the level of children's mathematics from their performance in preschool (age 5 to 6). The second purpose of the study was to test if children at-risk for mathematical learning disabilities in grade 1 (age 6 to 7) can be detected from their preparatory skills in preschool.

2.1.2. Participants

A total of 108 (54 girls, 54 boys) children participated in the pilot study. All children were tested in May of preschool (M=5.9 years, SD=4.0 months) and one year later in grade 1. The original 'nonselected' sample consisted of all the children (n= 108). For some analyses out of the original

---

[1] This section is based on Stock, P., Desoete, A., & Roeyers, H. (2007). Early markers for arithmetic difficulties. *Educational & Child Psychology, 24*, 28-39.

sample a smaller sample (*n*=67) of 'low achieving' (LA) and 'at least moderate achieving' (MA) Caucasian, native Dutch-speaking children, without a history of ADHD, sensory impairment, brain damage, chronic poor health, serious emotional or behavioral problems, or a poor educational background were selected. The LA-children (10 boys and 11 girls) performed below the 11th percentile on at least one standardized mathematical tests and the low mathematical performance level was confirmed by the form teacher of the child. The MA-children (22 boys and 24 girls) scored above the 50th percentile on both mathematical tests, had an age-appropriate performance level (at least level B; 60%) according to the form teacher and no signs of any learning disability. All children and parents were fluent native Dutch-speakers.

2.1.3. Measurement

The Kortrijk Arithmetic Test Revision (Kortrijkse Rekentest Revision, KRTR) (Baudonck et al., 2006) is a Belgian test on *mathematical reasoning* which requires that children solve mental arithmetic (e.g., 19-7=…) and number knowledge tasks (e.g., one less Early markers for mathematical difficulties 9 than eight is …). The psychometric value of the KRT-R has been demonstrated on a sample of 3,246 Dutch-speaking children from grade 1 to 6. In the study, the standardized total percentile based on Flanders norms was used.

The Arithmetic Number Facts test (Tempo Test Rekenen, TTR; de Vos, 1992) is a *numerical facility* test which requires that children in grade 1 solve as many number fact problems as possible within 2 minutes (e.g., 3+2=…). The psychometric value has been demonstrated for Flanders on a sample of 10,059 children (Ghesquière & Ruijssenaars, 1994).

TEDI-MATH (Grégoire et al., 2004 Flamish adaptation) is a test designed for the assessment of mathematical disabilities from preschool till grade 3. The psychometric value has been demonstrated on a sample of 550 Dutch speaking Belgian children and has been proven to be a well validated and reliable instrument (Desoete, 2006).

Pilot Study on Early Markers for Mathematical Difficulties 19

Procedural knowledge of counting is assessed using accuracy in counting numbers, counting forward to an upper bound (i.e., up to 6), counting forward from a lower bound (i.e., from 3), counting forward with an upper and lower bound (i.e., from 5 up to 9), counting forward by number (e.g., what number you get when you count five numbers on from eight), counting backward given a starting number (i.e., 7), and counting by step (i.e., by 2) from it. One point was given for a correct answer. A sum score was constructed (maximum: 14 points). Cronbach's alpha was .73.

Conceptual knowledge of counting is assessed with judgments about the validity of counting procedures. Children had to judge the counting of linear and random patterns of drawings and counters. To assess the abstraction principle, children had to count different kind of objects who were presented in a heap. Furthermore, a child who counted a set of objects was asked 'how many objects are there in total?', or 'how many objects are there if you start counting with the leftmost object in the array'. When children had to count again to answer they did not gain any points, as this was considered to represent good procedural knowledge but a lack of understanding of the counting principles of Gelman and Gallistel (1978). One point was given for a correct answer with a correct motivation. A sum score was constructed (maximum: 13 points). The Cronbach's alpha was .85.

Three *logical operations* were assessed. Children had to *seriate* numbers (e.g., 'Sort the cards from the one with fewer trees to the one with the most trees'; maximum: 3 points). The Cronbach's alpha for the subtest was .68. Children had to make groups of cards in order to assess the *classification* of numbers (e.g., 'Make groups with the cards that go together'; maximum: 3 points). The Cronbach's alpha was .73. Counters were used to test the *conservation* of numbers (e.g., " Do you have more counters than me? Do I have more counters than you? Or do we have the same number of counters? And why is this?; maximum: 4 points). One point was given for a correct answer with a correct logical motivation. The Cronbach's alpha was .85.

Magnitude comparison is assessed by comparison dot sets (6 items) and numbers (12 items). Preschool children and first graders were asked were they saw most dots. The first graders were also asked which number was closest to a certain target number. One point was given for a correct answer. A sum score was constructed (maximum: 6 points in preschool and 18 points in Grade 1). The Cronbach's alpha was .79.

2.2. RESULTS

The linear combination of the kindergarten abilities was significantly related to mathematical reasoning assessed in grade 1 (at age 6 to 7) with KRT, F (6, 107) = 18.659, $p \leq$ .0005. R^2 was .489. Especially conceptual counting knowledge and seriation was beneficial for beginning mathematical reasoning. The second multiple regression analyses pointed out that the linear combination of the kindergarten abilities at age 5 to 6 was also significantly related to numerical facility one year later (at age 6 to 7) assessed with TTR, F (6, 107) = 9.655, $p <$ .0005. R^2 was .327. Conceptual knowledge and seriation in preschool seem to be especially beneficial for both mathematical reasoning and numerical facility in grade 1.

The linear combination of kindergarten abilities was significantly related to mathematical reasoning in the same grade, F (6, 107) = 6.067, $p \leq$ .0005. R^2 was .221. The linear combination of kindergarten abilities was also significantly related to numerical facility in the same grade, and F (6, 107) = 3.056, $p \leq$ .009. R^2 was .103.

To answer the second research question, and to investigate if children at-risk for mathematical disabilities in grade 1 (age 6 to 7) can be detected by their kindergarten skills in preschool one year earlier, a discriminant analysis on the sample (n=67) of 'low achieving' (LA) and 'at least moderate achieving' (MA) Caucasian, native Dutch-speaking children.

Wilks' lambda was significant, Λ = .51, χ^2 (6, N = 67) = 41.54, $p \leq$ .0005, indicating that overall the predictors differentiated among the low achieving and the at least moderate achieving group. Conceptual knowledge of counting and seriation demonstrate the strongest relationships with initial mathematics.

The mean kindergarten scores on the discriminant function were consistent with this interpretation. The at least moderate achieving group did better on conditional knowledge and seriation than the low achieving group. Based on the scores for these six predictors, 86.6% was classified correctly into the low achieving of at least moderate achieving group, whereas 83.6% of the cross-validated grouped cases were classified correctly. Based on the six kindergarten scores 95.7% (or 44 out of the 46 children) of the at least moderate achievers and 66.7% of low achieving children (or 14 out of 21 children) were classified correctly.

2.3. Discussion of the Pilot Study

In this pilot study, we focused on the prediction of the level of children's mathematics in grade 1 from their performance in preschool, to add to our understanding of initial development mathematical skills and to help teachers focus on early markers for mathematical difficulties.

About half of the variance in mathematical reasoning skills in first grade can be predicted by assessing six kindergarten skills in preschool. Only about one fifth of the variance in mathematical reasoning skills can be predicted by assessing the same skills in grade 1. Three markers showed significant contributions: conceptual counting knowledge and seriation in preschool and procedural counting knowledge in grade 1. The current results also suggest that more then one third of the variance in numerical facility in grade 1 can be predicted by assessing skills in preschool. Only about one tenth of the variance is in fact due to retrieval skills that can be predicted by assessing the same skills in grade 1, although no individual markers were significant. The analysis on low and at least average performing first graders was consistent with the previous analysis. Two thirds of the lower-elementary school children classified as 'at risk' were classified correctly based on their performances in preschool at the age 5 to

6. Especially conceptual knowledge and seriation were suitable predictors of at-risk mathematical performance. In line with the research of Kingma (1983), the Piagetian model had some value added since children-at risk in grade 1 had lower scores on seriation tasks, compared with at least average performing peers. In line with Geary and Hoard (2005) children at-risk also had less developed counting knowledge and especially lacked conceptual counting knowledge. Moreover, in line with the idea of Rittle-Johnson and colleagues (2001) arguing that procedural knowledge and conceptual knowledge develop iteratively, we found weak connections between those components.

These results have as implication that in young children we should not only assess how accurate children can count (procedural knowledge) but also how they master the counting principles of Gallistel and Gelman (1992). It might be interesting to see if a controlled intervention focusing on conceptual counting knowledge and seriation skills in children at-risk can prevent learning difficulties from occurring later in these vulnerable children. Summarizing, our pilot study supports that we should assess procedural counting knowledge, the ability to seriate in preschool, and also the ability to distinguish essential form inessential counting characteristics (or the conceptual counting knowledge of young children).

Chapter 3

SCREENING FOR MATHEMATICAL DISABILITIES IN KINDERGARTEN: A CROSS-SECTIONAL STUDY[1]

3.1. METHOD

3.2.1. Participants

This study has been carried out utilizing a total group of 361 children (174 boys and 187 girls) in kindergarten. Children had a mean age of 70.25 months (*SD* = 3.99). Based on the numeric mathematical tests, smaller samples of 'low achieving' (LA) and 'at least moderately achieving' (MA) children were selected out of the original samples. LA-children performed below the 11th percentile on the mathematical mathematical abilities test. The MA-children scored above the 50th percentile on this numeric subtest. The LA-group consisted of 26 children, 167 children were selected as MA.

---

[1] This section is based on Stock, P., Desoete, A., & Roeyers, H. (2009b). Screening for mathematical disabilities in Kindergarten. *Developmental* Neurohabilitation, 12, 389-396.

3.2.2. Measurement

In order to have an estimate of the *numeric mathematical abilities* of the children we used a numeric subtest of the TEDI-MATH test battery (Grégoire, Noël, & Van Nieuwenhoven, 2004). The numeric mathematical abilities test consisted of a series of simple mathematical operations. First, the child was presented with six mathematical operations on pictures (e.g., 'Here you see two red balloons and three blue balloons. How many balloons are there together?'). One point was given for a correct answer (maximum: 6 points). Cronbach's alpha was .82. We also presented 18 simple additions presented visually and orally in arithmetic format (e.g. '9 + 4 = ...'). When the child made five mistakes, this subtest was interrupted. One point was given for a correct answer (maximum: 18 points). Cronbach's alpha for this set of items was .95. Finally, children had to solve some simple word problems (e.g. 'Dannie has two marbles. He wins two marbles. How many marbles does he have altogether now?'). This subtest was interrupted after the child made five mistakes. One point was given for a correct answer (maximum: 12 points). Cronbach's alpha was .84. The total raw item scores for this numeric mathematical abilities test were summed and converted to z-scores in order to analyse the results. This numeric arithmetic abilities test has proven to have good convergent and divergent validity (Desoete, 2006; 2007b).

Four *preparatory abilities* were assessed: procedural counting knowledge, conceptual counting knowledge, logical abilities and magnitude comparison. In order to assess these abilities some subtests of TEDI-MATH (Grégoire et al., 2004) were used.

3.2. RESULTS

A multivariate analysis of variance (MANOVA) was conducted to investigate whether children with low (LA) and at least moderate (MA) numeric mathematical abilities can be differentiated on their prenumeric abilities. Six prenumeric abilities were entered as dependent variables:

procedural counting knowledge, conceptual counting knowledge, seriation, classification, conservation and magnitude comparison. The MANOVA was significant on the multivariate level, $F (6, 186) = 29.73$, $p < .001$. On the univariate level there were significant differences between the groups for all six preparatory mathematical abilities. The MA group performed significantly better than the LA group on procedural counting knowledge, conceptual counting knowledge, seriation, classification, conservation and magnitude estimation.

In order to find out whether it was possible to classify children in the LA or the MA group based on procedural counting knowledge, conceptual counting knowledge, seriation, classification, conservation and magnitude comparison, a discriminant analysis procedure was performed. The Fisher's linear discriminant function was used to investigate the accurateness of the predicted classifications. The overall Wilks' lambda was significant, $\Lambda = .51$, $\chi^2 (6, N = 193) = 126.41$, $p < .001$, indicating that overall preparatory mathematical abilities differed among the LA and MA group. Procedural counting knowledge and seriation demonstrated the strongest relationships with mathematical abilities. Based on the scores for these six predictors, 93.8% of the children was classified correctly into the LA or MA group for mathematical abilities, whereas 92.7% of the cross-validated group cases were classified correctly. Based on the six preparatory mathematical abilities, 76.9% of low numeric achieving children and 96.4% of the at least moderately numeric achievers were classified correctly. In order to take into account chance agreement, a kappa coefficient was computed and obtained a value of .73, indicating a good prediction.

3.3. DISCUSSION OF STUDY 2

With a cross-sectional design we looked for differences in these preparatory mathematical abilities between children who were low achieving or at least moderately achieving in numeric mathematics. The results showed that there were indeed important differences in the preparatory mathematical abilities. Children who were low achieving in numeric mathematics did significantly worse on procedural counting, conceptual counting, seriation, classification, conservation and magnitude comparison tasks than children who had at least moderate scores in numeric mathematics. Based on these six preparatory mathematical abilities, more than ninety percent of children could be classified correctly as low achieving or at least moderately achieving in numeric mathematics. Particularly, procedural counting knowledge and seriation seemed to have an important role in the prediction of mathematical abilities. The classification results for the at least moderately achieving children were better than the classification results for low achieving children, but more than three of four children with weak numeric abilities could be detected based on the preparatory mathematical abilities.

Our results outline the important role of counting knowledge, logical abilities and magnitude comparison in the development of numeric mathematical abilities, even in kindergarten. In line with Geary and Hoard (2005) low achieving children also had less developed counting knowledge. Evidence was found for weaker performances on both procedural and conceptual counting tasks. These results indicate that it is not only important to assess how accurate young children can count (procedural knowledge) but also how they master the counting principles of Gallistel and Gelman (1992; conceptual counting knowledge). The Piagetian model had some value added since low achieving children had lower scores than at least moderately achieving children on seriation, classification and conservation tasks. In line with Stock and colleagues (2007, 2010), seriation demonstrated to be a possible important prenumeric marker. Furthermore, this study confirmed the findings of Landerl and colleagues (2004) that low achieving children did worse on magnitude comparison tasks than at least average performing peers.

Summarizing, the results indicated that kindergartners with low numeric mathematical performances tend to have lower scores on preparatory mathematical tasks than children who are at least moderately achieving in numeric mathematics. Evidence was found for differences in procedural counting knowledge, conceptual counting knowledge, seriation, classification, conservation and magnitude comparison abilities. These preparatory arithmetic abilities can be seen as basic stones for the later numeric arithmetic development and could possibly serve as powerful early markers in the detection or screening of arithmetic disabilities. Preparatory arithmetic abilities may provide additional longitudinal predictions regarding mathematics. Kindergarten tests should therefore include these aspects.

Chapter 4

MASTERY OF COUNTING PRINCIPLES IN TODDLERS: A LONGITUDINAL STUDY[1]

4.1. METHOD

4.1.1. Participants

This study has been carried out in a total group of 423 children, 200 boys and 223 girls. All children were Caucasian native Dutch-speaking children living in the Flemish part of Belgium. The children were tested in the second part of the school year (April or May) in the last kindergarten class and again in the same period when they were in first grade. Children who received professional treatment for learning or other disabilities were excluded from the sample.

---

[1] Based on Stock, P., Desoete, A., & Roeyers, H. (2009). Mastery of Counting Principles Principles in Toddlers: A Crucial Step in the Development of Budding Arithmetic Abilities? *Learning and Individual Differences*, *19*, 419-422.

4.2.2. Measurement

All children were tested in kindergarten on their knowledge of counting principles. A follow-up assessment with two mathematical tests was conducted in first grade. All counting abilities were tested with different items of the TEDI-MATH (Grégoire, Noel, & Van Nieuwenhoven, 2004). Mastery of three counting principles was assessed: the stable order principle, the one-one-correspondence principle and the cardinality principle.

Mastery of the stable order principle was assessed using accuracy in counting numbers. Children had to count up to 30. Children earned two points when they could count faultlessly in the first attempt, one point was earned when two attempts were necessary. Children were further asked to count forward with an upper bound (one point) and with a lower bound (one point). Children who gained three or more points on these items were classified as mastering the stable order principle.

Mastery of the one-one-correspondence principle was assessed using accuracy in counting linear and random patterns of drawings. Children were asked to count, for example, all the rabbits on a drawing. Four items were presented, one point was given for every correct answer. Children who gained three or more points on these items were classified as mastering the one-one-correspondence principle.

Mastery of the cardinality principle was assessed with a so-called 'how many'-task (Wynn, 1990; 1992). This kind of task requires responding with the last number word of the counting sequence and fits well with the cardinality principle as postulated by Gelman and Gallistel (1978; Bermejo, Morales, & Osuna, 2004). After presenting the counting items as described for measurement of the one-one-correspondence, children were asked 'How many are there in total?'. Four items were presented, one point was given for every correct answer. Children who gained three or more points on these items were classified as mastering the cardinality principle.

In order to have a full perspective on the mathematical abilities of children in first grade, two mathematical tests were used: The Kortrijk

Arithmetic Test Revised (Kortrijkse Rekentest Revision, KRT-R, Baudonck et al., 2006) and the Arithmetic Number Facts test (Tempo Test Rekenen, TTR, De Vos, 1992).

4.3. RESULTS

4.3.1. Mastery of Counting Abilities in Kindergarten

In this sample 62.4% of children mastered the stable order rinciple, 95.3% mastered the one-one-correspondence principle and 65.7% mastered the cardinality principle. Only 44.2% of children mastered all three counting principles by the end of kindergarten.

4.3.2. Prediction of Mathematical Abilities

The second hypothesis was that the scores on the mathematical tests in first grade could be predicted based on the counting scores in kindergarten. The results of intraclass correlation indicate that between 40 and 50% of the variance in the dependent variables could be explained by the cluster structure of the data, meaning that going to the same school tends to exert an influence on scores on mathematical tests.

Multilevel analyses were performed with counting skills as the independent predictor for mathematical achievement and numerical facility respectively. The scores on the mathematical tests were treated at Level 1 and classrooms were classified as Level 2. In the fixed part of the model we see that children with better counting skills in kindergarten tended to perform better on mathematical tests in first grade. The individual level intercept variance is .56 for mathematical achievement and .63 for numerical facility. The classroom level intercept variance is .57 for mathematical achievement and .42 for numerical facility. The random part of the model shows that classrooms differ in their mean performances. Yet no significant slope variance was found for the scores on the mathematical tests between the different classrooms.

4.4. DISCUSSION OF STUDY 3

The results showed that almost all children had a thorough command of the one-one-correspondence principle. In contrast to the existing literature (Briars & Siegler, 1984; Freeman et al., 2000; Gelman & Meck, 1983; Le Fevre et al., 2006; Wynn, 1992) the results pointed out that not all children in the dataset mastered the other two essential counting principles by the end of kindergarten. Concerning the stable order principle it was found that about sixty percent of children mastered this principle by the end of the last kindergarten class. Finally, about two thirds of children in the last kindergarten class could apply the cardinality principle when counting. This finding is in contrast to the findings that the understanding of the cardinality principle is the most difficult principle, developing relatively late (Butterworth, 2004; Fuson, 1988). The results showed that almost one third of children still had problems with understanding the stable order or the cardinality principle. More than half of children did not master the three counting principles by the end of kindergarten. Big differences in the mastery of the essential counting principles in toddlers existed, so teachers should give added attention to the different skill levels children bring with them when entering first grade.

In addition, the better children performed on the counting items in the last kindergarten class, the better they performed on the two mathematical tests in first grade. Based on the counting scores of children at the end of the last kindergarten class, fourteen percent of the variance in the scores for mathematical achievement in first grade could be explained. These results confirm the important role of counting abilities in the development of proficient mathematical strategies (Blöte et al., 2006; Le Fevre et al., 2006; Stock et al., 2007).

In addition, significant proportions of the variance in the scores for the number fact test in first grade could be explained, but this proportion was limited to only five percent. Although earlier research also stressed the role of counting abilities in the automatisation of arithmetic facts (Aunola et al., 2004; Van de Rijt & Van Luit, 1999), it was found that mastery of the essential counting principles was far more important to the command of mental arithmetics and number knowledge than for the automatisation of arithmetic facts.

In conclusion we can say that less than half of all children in Flanders mastered the three essential counting principles: the stable order, the one-one-correspondence and the cardinality principle by the end of kindergarten. Therefore, teachers in first grade should give sufficient attention to this great variety in counting abilities when children start basic schooling. Our results revealed that mastery of the counting principles in kindergarten was predictive for scores on mathematical tests one year later in first grade. It was possible to explain significant proportions of scores on mathematical tests in first grade based on the counting scores in kindergarten, this was especially the case for mathematical achievement tests. Yet there were important differences between schools but the relationships between counting scores and scores on mathematics tests one year later were stable. Taking into account the large differences in counting skills children bring with them when starting basic schooling and the fact that scores on counting tasks were good predictors for later mathematical abilities, it is important that teachers in first grade give sufficient attention to the instruction of counting skills.

Chapter 5

DETECTING CHILDREN WITH DISABILITIES IN KINDERGARTEN? LONGITUDINAL STUDY 4[1]

5.1. METHOD

5.1.1. Participants

This study has been carried out in a total group of 684 children (350 boys and 334 girls). All children were Caucasian native Dutch-speaking children living in the Flemish part of Belgium. A group of 308 children was tested for the first time in October or November of the last kindergarten class (mean age 64.87 months, SD 3.86 months). We indicated this group as cohort one. The second group (labeled as cohort two) consisted of 376 children who were tested for the first time in April or May of the last kindergarten class (mean age 70.26 months, SD 4.00 months). Taking into account the speed of development in young children causing important developmental differences between those two cohorts, we analyzed the results of the two cohorts separately.

---

[1] This section is based on Stock, P., Desoete, A., & Roeyers, H. (2009). Predicting Arithmetic Abilities: The Role of Preparatory Arithmetic Markers and Intelligence. *Journal of Psychoeducational Assessment*, 27, 237-251.

5.1.2. Measurement

In order to assess the preparatory mathematical abilities, some subtests of the TEDI-MATH (Grégoire, Noël, & Van Nieuwenhoven, 2004) were used. In order to have a full outlook on the mathematical abilities of children in first and second grade, two mathematical tests were used: The Kortrijk Arithmetic Test Revised (Kortrijkse Rekentest Revision, KRT-R, Baudonck et al., 2006) and the Arithmetic Number Facts test (Tempo Test Rekenen, TTR, De Vos, 1992). The combination of the TTR and an earlier version of the KRT-R were found to be reliable in order to have an acurate appraisal of children's mathematical abilities (Desoete, Roeyers, & De Clercq, 2004).

In order to have an estimation of the intellectual capacities of the child a short version of the Wechsler Intelligence Scale for Children, third edition (Wechsler, 1991 - WISC-III) was assessed. The short version was based on four subtests and included both measures for crystallized and fluid intelligence (Vocabulary, Similarities, Block Design and Picture Arrangement; Grégoire, 2001).

5.2. RESULTS

In order to take into account any developmental differences, results of children tested in the beginning of the last kindergarten class (cohort one) and children tested at the end of the same year (cohort two) were analyzed separately.

5.2.1. Prediction of Mathematical Abilities in First Grade

Two multiple regression analysis were conducted in order to evaluate the preparatory mathematical abilities and intelligence predicted numerical facility and mathematical reasoning in the beginning of first grade (cohort one). Five predictors were included: procedural knowledge of counting, conceptual knowledge of counting, seriation, classification and intelligence. The linear combination of the predictors was significantly related to numerical facility in first grade, $F (5, 200) = 7.57$, $p < .001$ and mathematical reasoning in first grade, $F (5, 200) = 9.18$, $p < .001$. Approximately 16% of the variance in numerical facility and 19% of the variance in mathematical reasoning in the sample could be accounted for by the linear combination of the five predictors. Seriation and classification had a significant contribution to both numerical facility and mathematical reasoning while procedural counting abilities only had a significant contribution to mathematical reasoning in the beginning of first grade (cohort one).

Two other multiple regression analysis were conducted in order to evaluate how well the preparatory mathematical abilities and intelligence predicted numerical facility and mathematical reasoning at the end of first grade (cohort two). The same predictors were included and conservation was added as a sixth predictor. The linear combination of the predictors was significantly related to numerical facility, $F (6,257) = 4.03$, $p < .001$ and mathematical reasoning, $F (6,257) = 14.57$, $p < .001$. Approximately 9% of the variance in numerical facility and 26% of the variance in mathematical reasoning in the sample could be accounted for by the linear combination of the six predictors. Seriation had a significant contribution to both numerical facility and mathematical reasoning while intelligence only had a significant contribution to mathematical reasoning at the end of first grade (cohort two).

5.2.2. Prediction of Mathematical Abilities in Second Grade

Two multiple regression analysis were conducted in order to evaluate how well preparatory mathematical abilities and intelligence predicted numerical facility and mathematical reasoning in the beginning of second grade (cohort one). Again five predictors were included: procedural knowledge of counting, conceptual knowledge of counting, seriation, classification and intelligence. The linear combination of the predictors was significantly related to numerical facility in second grade, $F (5, 199) = 3.50$, $p < .01$ and mathematical reasoning in first grade, $F (5, 200) = 21.98$, $p < .001$. Approximately 8% of the variance in numerical facility and 36% of the variance in mathematical reasoning in the sample could be accounted for by the linear combination of the predictors. Procedural counting knowledge and seriation had a significant contribution to numerical facility in the beginning of second grade (cohort one). In the prediction of mathematical reasoning in that same period, procedural counting knowledge, intelligence and classification had a significant impact.

Another two multiple regression analysis was conducted in order to evaluate how well the preparatory mathematical abilities and intelligence predicted numerical facility and mathematical reasoning at the end of second grade (cohort two). The same predictors were included and conservation was added as a sixth predictor. The linear combination of the predictors was significantly related to numerical facility, $F (6, 277) = 2.90$, $p < .01$ and mathematical reasoning, $F (6, 282) = 5.84$, $p < .001$. Approximately 6% of the variance in numerical facility and 11% of the variance in mathematical reasoning in the sample could be accounted for by the linear combination of the six predictors. Only procedural counting knowledge had a significant contribution to numerical facility and only intelligence had a significant contribution to mathematical reasoning at the end of second grade (cohort two).

5.3. DISCUSSION OF STUDY 4

Based on preparatory mathematical abilities in kindergarten and intelligence, about one sixth of the variance in numerical facility and one fifth of the variance in mathematical reasoning in the beginning of first grade could be explained. Based on preparatory mathematical abilities and intelligence, more than one third of variance in mathematical reasoning in the beginning of second grade could be explained. Preparatory mathematical abilities had a growing impact in the prediction of mathematical reasoning, while the role of those early kindergarten markers in predicting numerical facility decreased. In addition, although strong indications were found that seriation and procedural counting knowledge serve as the most important markers, the analysis have not consistently pointed out one specific predictor or a recurrent combination of predictors. Based on these findings it is recommended to assess a set of markers including logic thinking abilities, like seriation and classification and counting knowledge, when predictions of later mathematical abilities needs to be made.

Taken together, when looking for predictions of mathematical abilities, it is advised to assess in kindergarten a set of preparatory mathematical abilities including logic thinking abilities and counting knowledge. Furthermore, it is important to take into account intelligence when looking for useful predictors for mathematical reasoning. Our results highlight that performances on preparatory mathematical abilities and intelligence are not completely determinative of later mathematical abilities in children. The preparatory markers are very useful for the early detection of children who are at risk for developing mathematical disabilities, but much flexibility in childhood development remains. These findings should encourage teachers and clinicians to track and motivate children with weak preparatory mathematical skills.

Chapter 6

STUDY 5[1]

6.1. METHOD

6.1.1. Participants

This study has been carried out in a total group of 471 children (227 boys and 244 girls). All children were Caucasian native Dutch-speaking children living in the Flemish part of Belgium. In Belgium, children attend kindergarten class for about three years and move to elementary classes in the year that they turn six year old. A group of 213 children was tested for the first time at the beginning of the last kindergarten class (October or November, mean age 64.80 months, *SD* 3.70 months), 258 children were tested for the first time at the end of the last kindergarten class (April or May, mean age 70.33 months, *SD* 3.84 months). Sixteen children were excluded from the sample because their intellectual capacities were not in the normal range of 85-115. Children were classified as having Mathematical Disabilities (MD) if they scored below the 11th percentile on at least one of the mathematical achievement tests, both in first and second grade (*n* = 17). Children who scored between the 10th and 25th percentiles

---

[1] Partially based on Stock, P., Desoete, A., & Roeyers, H. (2009). Detecting children with arithmetic disabilities from kindergarten. Evidence from a three year longitudinal study on the role of preparatory arithmetic abilities, *Journal of Learning disabilities, 43*, 250-268.

on at least one of the mathematical achievement tests, both in first and second grade, were classified as low achieving (LA; $n = 61$). This group also included children who scored below the 11th percentile in first or second grade and who scored between the 10th and 25th percentiles in the other year. The third group consisted of children who scored above the 25th percentile on all mathematical achievement tests in both grades, these children were classified as typical achievers (TA, $n = 216$). Finally 161 children did not meet one of these criteria and were not included in the analysis. Socio-economic status was derived from the total number of years of scholarship of the parents (starting from the beginning of elementary school). No significant differences in SES were found between the MD, LA and TA groups for the number of years of scholarship of mothers and 6 for the number of years of scholarship of fathers.

6.1.2. Assessment

All children were tested in kindergarten on their preparatory mathematical abilities.

A follow-up assessment with two mathematical tests was conducted in first and second grade, and intellectual abilities were tested in second grade.

All preparatory mathematical abilities were tested with different subtests of the TEDIMATH (Grégoire, Noel, & Van Nieuwenhoven, 2004).

In first and second grade, two mathematical tests were used: The Kortrijk Arithmetic Test Revised (Kortrijkse Rekentest Revision, KRT-R, Baudonck et al., 2006) and the Arithmetic Number Facts Test (Tempo Test Rekenen, TTR, De Vos, 1992).

In order to have an estimation of the intellectual capacities of the children, a short version of the Wechsler Intelligence Scale for Children, third edition (Wechsler, 1991 - WISC-III) was assessed. This is the most recent form in Flanders at the moment. The short version is based on four subtests and includes both measures for crystallized and fluid intelligence

(Vocabulary, Similarities, Block Design and Picture Arrangement; Grégoire, 2001).

6.2. RESULTS

6.2.1. Group Differences in Preparatory Mathematical and Intellectual Abilities

A multivariate analysis of variance (MANOVA) was conducted to investigate the differences between the Mathematical Disabilities (MD), Low Achieving (LA) and Typically Achieving (TA) group on six dependent variables: procedural counting knowledge, conceptual counting knowledge, seriation, classification, magnitude comparison (assessed in kindergarten) and intellectual abilities. The MANOVA was significant on the multivariate level, $F (12, 568) = 6.02$, $p < .001$.

On the univariate level there were significant differences between the groups for procedural counting knowledge, conceptual counting knowledge, seriation, classification and magnitude comparison, but not for intelligence. Post hoc Bonferonni analysis revealed that the TA group performed significantly better than the MD group on conceptual counting knowledge and significantly better than the LA and MD group on procedural counting knowledge, seriation and classification. The scores for magnitude comparison were significantly different for the three groups with the TA group performing the best and the MD group performing the worst.

6.2.2. Prediction of Group Membership

A discriminant analysis procedure was conducted on the selected group with only the children in the MD, LA and TA group. The overall Wilks' lambda was significant, $\Lambda = .79$, $\chi^2 (12, N = 292) = 68.59$, $p < .001$, indicating, that overall, the kindergarten predictors differentiated among the MD, LA and TA group. Magnitude comparison, seriation and classification demonstrated the strongest relationships with general mathematical achievement of the children.

The means on the discriminant function were consistent with this interpretation. The TA for mathematical abilities did better on the preparatory mathematical abilities. Based on the scores for these four predictors, 73.3% was classified correctly into the MD, LA or TA group for general mathematical achievement, whereas 71.6% of the cross-validated grouped cases were classified correctly. Based on the six predictors only 29.4% of children had mathematical disabilities, 4.9% of LA children and 96.3% of the TA children were classified correctly. In order to take into account chance agreement, a kappa coefficient was computed and obtained a value of .17, indicating a weak prediction.

6.3. DISCUSSION

Children with mathematical disabilities did significantly worse on conceptual counting tasks than typically achieving children. No significant differences were found between the children who were low achieving in mathematics and typically achieving children or children with mathematical disabilities. Concerning performance on procedural counting knowledge, seriation and classification, no significant differences were found between the children with mathematical disabilities and the low achieving children, but both groups performed significantly worse than typically achieving children. Finally, there were significant differences between the three groups in magnitude comparison, with children with mathematical disabilities performing the worst and typically achieving children performing the best.

The results showed that different conclusions can be drawn when using samples with children with mathematical disabilities or samples with low achieving children and that the operationalisation of the retardation criterion is determinative for the results. Children with mathematical disabilities did indeed perform worse on all investigated preparatory mathematical abilities, but this was not the case for children who were low achieving in mathematics. Low achieving children did not perform significantly worse on conceptual counting knowledge than typically achieving peers and magnitude comparison was found to be the only kindergarten preparatory mathematical ability that could discriminate between all three groups. These results illustrate that it is important to include conceptual counting and magnitude comparison tasks in kindergarten assessment batteries that aim to detect children at risk for developing mathematical disabilities. The significant differences in the performances on the magnitude comparison task between the three groups strengthen the idea that this could be a core deficit in children with mathematical disabilities (Butterworth, 2005; Gersten et al., 2005; Holloway & Ansari, 2008; Landerl et al., 2004). Furthermore, the current analysis demonstrated that low achieving children and children with mathematical disabilities show different mathematical profiles in kindergarten. This supports the fact that results of low achievers can not automatically be implemented for children with mathematical disabilities. Since the criteria used to define children with mathematical disabilities in the current study approach the criteria used in clinical practice, this also indicates that clinicians have to be careful with conclusions of scientific studies that used a more lenient criterion.

The second purpose of this study was to determine if it was possible to detect children with mathematical disabilities based on the preparatory mathematical abilities measured in kindergarten. It was found that more than 70 percent of the children could be classified correctly into the mathematical disabilities, low achieving or typically achieving group based on the kindergarten preparatory mathematical abilities. Magnitude comparison, seriation and classification demonstrated the strongest relationship with the general mathematical achievement of the children. These results again outline that it is important to include magnitude comparison measures in assessment batteries that aim to detect kindergartners who are at risk for mathematical disabilities. Furthermore, the Piagetian model proved to add some value, since it was shown that difficulties with seriation and classification tasks can serve as indication for an at risk mathematics development. Finally, intellectual abilities had no important influence on the predictions, indicating that the problems children with mathematical disabilities encounter can not be reduced to lower intellectual abilities.

Yet, we have to be careful with conclusions on the classification results. Almost all children who were observed as typically achieving in mathematics were classified as such, but the percentage of correct classifications was much lower for the mathematical disabilities and the low achieving group, with about 30 and 5 percent respectively. It was found that, based on the preparatory mathematical abilities, children in the arithmetic disabilities group were classified as typical achievers more than 60 percent of the time. Low achieving children were misclassified as typically achieving more than 80 percent of the time and as having mathematical disabilities more than 10 percent of the time. The results of these analyses demonstrated relatively good specificity but low sensitivity, concluding that it was difficult to detect children with mathematical disabilities based on only the preparatory mathematical abilities in kindergarten.

Chapter 7

GENERAL DISCUSSION

Early mathematical abilities have been found to be the strongest predictors of later school achievement (Duncan et al., 2007). If markers for the mathematical development can be recognised, it might be possible to prevent children who are at risk for developing mathematical disabilities from falling further behind (Gersten, Jordan, & Flojo, 2005; Pasnak, Cooke, & Hendricks, 2006). The principal goal of these studies was to investigate the role of preparatoryı mathematical abilities in the prediction of later mathematical performances in a large group of children with a broad range of mathematical abilities.

First of all, we focused on the Piagetian logical abilities, such as seriation, classification and conservation. Piaget and Szeminska (1941) suggested a relationship between seriation and classification and the understanding of numbers. In 1959, Piaget and Inhelder stated that the coordination of seriation and classification is needed for the comprehension that '4' is included in '5', whereas '5' itself is included in '6' (Grégoire, 2005). Since the publication of the Piaget's work, several neo-Piagetian researchers have questioned the causality of seriation and classification for understanding numbers (e.g., Dumont, 1994; Lourenço & Machado, 1996) and stressed schooling as a powerful factor responsible for producing cognitive development (Cahan, Greenbaum, Artman, Deluya & Gappel-Gilon, 2008). Nevertheless, other studies revealed that seriation assessed in kindergarten is related to mathematical achievement in grade 1 (e.g., Grégoire, 2005; Kingsma, 1984) and grade 2 (Grégoire, 2005); children adequately solving classification tasks in kindergarten performed better in mathematical tasks in grade 1 and 2 (Grégoire, 2005).

Besides the logical abilities, we also analysed post-Piagetian counting knowledge.

It is obvious that early mathematics involves counting (Barrouillet & Lepine, 2005; Wynn, 1990). Although a great deal of research looked into counting as a unitary ability, Dowker (2005) suggested that counting knowledge consists of procedural and conceptual aspects. It has been suggested that children's basic conceptual understanding of how to count objects and their knowledge of the order of numbers play an important role in mathematical performance because they promote the automatic use of mathematics-related information, allowing attentional resources to be devoted to more complex mathematical problem solving (Aunola, Leskinen, Lerkkanen, & Nurmi, 2004).

Finally we analysed the magnitude comparison skills of children. Deficiencies in depicting or accessing magnitude information are considered by some researchers as 'low level' symptoms consistent with the core deficit theory. Nevertheless, the same researchers acknowledge that higher level symptoms (impairments in acquisition of counting and addition procedures and fact retrieval) may be a derivative of an initial dysfunction of the core number sense system, even though there may be other possible causes of these high-level symptoms (Geary, Hoard, & Hamson, 1999; Xu & Spelke, 2000).

In this final discussion, we will summarize and discuss the main findings of the analyses presented. Furthermore, limitations of the studies will be formulated and future research challenges will be proposed. Finally, we will conclude with the implications of this work.

7.1. MAIN FINDINGS

The *pilot study* investigated whether it was possible to predict the level of 108 children's mathematical reasoning and numerical facility skills in first grade from their performances in kindergarten. About half of the variance in mathematical reasoning scores in first grade could be predicted by assessing seriation, classification and conservation; procedural and conceptual counting knowledge; and magnitude comparison skills in kindergarten. Only about one-fifth of the variance in mathematical reasoning abilities could be predicted by assessing the same predictors in first grade. Three markers showed significant contributions: conceptual counting knowledge and seriation in kindergarten, and procedural counting knowledge in first grade. The results also suggested that more than one-third of the variance in numerical facility scores in first grade could be predicted by assessing the preparatory mathematical abilities in kindergarten. Only about one-tenth of the variance in fact retrieval abilities could be predicted by assessing the same predictors in first grade, although no individual markers were significant. It was further tested whether children at risk for mathematical disabilities in first grade could be detected by their preparatory mathematical abilities in kindergarten. Two-thirds of the at-risk children were classified correctly based on their preparatory performances in kindergarten. Particularly, conceptual counting knowledge and seriation were suitable kindergarten predictors of at-risk mathematical performance in first grade. Although not significant, at-risk children also did worse on magnitude comparison tasks than at least average performing peers.

In *study 2* we focused on a cross-sectional design on the preparatory mathematical abilities, like counting knowledge, logical abilities and magnitude comparison, of kindergartners who were low achieving ($\leq$ pc 10); and at least moderately achieving (> pc 50) on numerical mathematical abilities like simple additions. The results showed that there were indeed important differences in the preparatory mathematical abilities between both groups. Numerical low achievers did significantly worse on seriation, classification, conservation, procedural counting, conceptual counting and magnitude comparison tasks than at least moderately achieving children. More than ninety percent of children could be classified correctly as low or at least moderate achievers. Seriation and procedural counting knowledge were principally important predictors. Furthermore, it was found that more than three of out of four children with poor numeric mathematical abilities could be detected based on their preparatory mathematical abilities.

The research in study 3 focused on counting principles. Since mastery of the essential counting principles has been described as an essential feature for the development of counting (Geary, 2004; Gelman & Meck, 1983; Wynn, 1992), we focused on only these three essential counting principles. Mastery of the stable order, the one-one correspondence and the cardinality principle in kindergarten was assessed in a group of 423 children with a broad range of mathematical abilities. In line with Geary, Bow-Thomas and Yao (1992), the frequency of mastery of the essential counting principles was examined in kindergartners. The results showed that almost all children had a thorough command of the one-one correspondence principle, but not all children mastered the other two essential counting principles by the end of kindergarten. Almost one-third of children still had problems with understanding the stable order or the cardinality principle. More than half the children did not master the three counting principles by the end of kindergarten. Furthermore, the relationship between counting abilities in kindergartners and their mathematical abilities in first grade was analyzed. Since the children were clustered in classrooms and an important amount of variance in the dependent variables could be explained by the cluster structure of the data, multilevel analyses were used. It was found that the better children performed on the counting items in the last kindergarten class, the better they performed on the mathematical reasoning and the numerical facility test in first grade. Based on the counting scores of children at the end of the last kindergarten class, fourteen percent of the variance in the scores for mathematical reasoning in first grade could be explained. In addition, significant proportions of the variance in the scores for the numerical facility test in first grade could be explained, but this proportion was limited to only five percent. In line with Opdenakker and Van Damme (2006), it was found that an important part of the variance (between 17 and 19 percent) in mathematical achievement in first grade could be associated with differences between schools. We found significant random variation for the mean class achievement, indicating that the level of performance was quite different between schools and that children sharing a common educational background tended to have more similar scores on mathematical tests when compared with children in other schools. Yet there was no random slope variation, meaning that the importance of mastery of the essential counting principles in the prediction of later mathematical achievement was the same for all classrooms. There was no differential influence of the school context on the basic counting knowledge of the children.

In *study 4*, a three-year longitudinal study on 684 children who were followed from kindergarten through second grade was presented. It was examined whether it was possible to predict the level of children's mathematical abilities in first and second grade from their performance in kindergarten on preparatory mathematical abilities like procedural counting knowledge, conceptual counting knowledge, seriation, classification and conservation.

Furthermore, since it was found that intelligence might be an important predictor for individual differences in scholastic achievement (Colom & Flores-Mendoza, 2007; Spinath, Spinath, Harlaar, & Plomin, 2006), the role of intelligence in mathematical reasoning and numerical facility was investigated. In addition, to obtain insight into the development of mathematical abilities during the school year, two cohorts of children, one in the beginning of every school year and one at the end of every school year, were investigated. The results pointed out that rather good predictions of mathematical abilities in first and second grade could be made based on preparatory mathematical abilities and intelligence. The proportion of predicted variance was very similar for both numerical facility and mathematical reasoning. From the second half of first grade on, a different picture surfaced, with large differences in the proportion of explained variance in numerical facility or mathematical reasoning. The preparatory abilities predicted better the mathematical reasoning skills than numerical facility. It could be possible that numerical facility is more dependent on the extent to which children are encouraged to exercise and automatize the retrieval of arithmetic facts. The prediction of both numerical facility and mathematical reasoning was rather weak at the end of second grade. Preparatory mathematical abilities and intelligence were included as possible important markers. Concerning the preparatory mathematical abilities, no unifying conclusion could be drawn. Although strong indications were found that seriation and procedural counting knowledge served as the most important markers, the analyses have not consistently pointed out one specific predictor or a recurrent combination of predictors. In line with former research (Colom & Flores-Mendoza, 2007; Spinath et al., 2006), the results further showed that intelligence had a significant contribution in the prediction of mathematical abilities in first and second grade, but this was very specific to mathematical reasoning and not for numerical facility. Based on the longitudinal study presented in study 4, children were selected as having mathematical disabilities or as low achieving or typically achieving in mathematics. Children were classified as having mathematical disabilities if they scored $\leq$ pc 10 on at least one of the mathematical achievement tests, both in first and second grade. The low achieving group consisted of children who scored between the 10th and 25th percentiles on at least one of the mathematical achievement tests, both in first and second grade. Finally, typical achievers scored above the 25th percentile on all mathematical achievement tests in both grades.

In *study 5* it was investigated whether it was possible to find group differences in Piagetian logical abilities, neo-Piagetian counting knowledge and performances on magnitude comparison tasks between these three groups of children. The analyses showed that significant differences in the performance on procedural counting knowledge, conceptual counting knowledge, seriation, classification and magnitude comparison could be found between children who had poor mathematicalperformances in first and second grade and children who were typically achieving. However, the differences found varied in function of the criteria used to define children with poor mathematical abilities. Children with mathematical disabilities and children who were low achieving on mathematical tests had different profiles. Children with mathematical disabilities did worse on all investigated preparatory mathematical abilities, but this was not the case for children who were low achieving in mathematics. Low achieving children did not perform significantly worse on conceptual counting knowledge than typically achieving peers, and magnitude comparison was found to be the only kindergarten preparatory mathematical ability that could discriminate between the three groups. The second purpose of this study was to determine whether it was possible to detect children with mathematical disabilities based on the preparatory mathematical abilities measured in kindergarten. It was found that more than 70 percent of the children could be classified correctly based on kindergarten preparatory mathematical abilities. Magnitude comparison, seriation, and classification demonstrated the strongest relationship with the general mathematical achievement of the children, while intellectual abilities had no important influence on the predictions. Almost all children who were observed as typically achieving in mathematics were classified as such, but the percentage of correct classifications was much lower for the mathematical disabilities and the low achieving group. Based on the preparatory abilities, children in the mathematical disabilities group were classified as typical achievers more than 60 percent of the time. Low achieving children were misclassified as typically achieving more than 80 percent of the time and as having mathematical disabilities more than 10 percent of the time. The results of these analyses demonstrated relatively good specificity but low sensitivity, leading to the conclusion that it was difficult to detect children with mathematical disabilities based only on their preparatory mathematics abilities in kindergarten.

7.2. COVERING CONCLUSIONS

7.2.1. Children's Mathematical Deficiencies when Starting Formal Schooling

Whereas it was supposed that most children would master the counting principles when they entered formal schooling (Briars & Siegler, 1984; Freeman, Antonucci, & Lewis, 2000; Gelman & Meck, 1983; Le Fevre et al., 2006; Wynn, 1992), this clearly was contradicted by the findings of the study in chapter 4. This study investigated performances on rather simple and basic counting tasks. Even children six years old did not always understand the counting principles that underlie their counting activities. Only about 40 percent of children mastered the three counting principles, revealing that children have a great variety of preparatory mathematical abilities when they enter elementary school. The study on the (preparatory) mathematical abilities of children in kindergarten forms a second argument that even before the start of formal schooling, different groups of typically or low achieving children could be outlined. These arguments feed the first conclusion of this project that children indeed have different mathematical skills when starting formal schooling, and that this is even the case for simple basic mathematical abilities that supposedly require no formal schooling.

7.2.2. Identifying Markers for Later Mathematical Abilities

From a cognitive framework, Piaget postulated that logical abilities like seriation, conservation and classification are conditional to the development of mathematical abilities (Piaget & Szeminska, 1941). This theory implies that these logical abilities are powerful predictors for later mathematical abilities. Based on the studies in this book, and in agreement with Grégoire (2005), we indeed found confirmation that the logical abilities as described in the Piagetian model had some value in the prediction of later mathematical abilities. Seriation was of major

General Discussion
55

importance in the prediction of mathematical abilities in all studies. Fyrthermore, we found sporadic evidence for a minor role of classification abilities (in the studies reported in study 4 and 5), whereas in our dataset conservation had no significant role in the prediction of later mathematical abilities. The results further strengthen the finding that, though a great deal of criticism has been formulated on the theory of Piaget (Lourenço & Machado, 1996), the logical abilities as described by Piaget do have an important role in the development of mathematical abilities. Like Grégoire (2005), who found that children who were successful in logical ability tasks performed better on mathematical tests; and mastery of seriation abilities had the strongest predictive power. Our findings further support the hypothesis that seriation can serve as a powerful predictor for later mathematical abilities.

The neo-Piagetian researchers questioned the importance of logical abilities and unilaterally focused on counting as a milestone in the development of later mathematical abilities (e.g., Aunola et al., 2004; Fuson, 1988; Le Corre Van de Walle, Brannon, & Carey , 2006). Based on our studies, we found confirmation for the theories that put the importance of counting abilities in the forefront. The results confirmed the role of counting abilities as a marker for the development of proficient mathematical strategies (Aunola et al., 2004; Blöte, Lieffering, & Ouwehand, 2006; Gersten et al., 2005; Le Fevre et al., 2006). In line with Geary and Hoard (2005), low achieving children also had less-developed counting abilities. Yet, varying findings on the importance of procedural and conceptual counting knowledge were found. Evidence was found for weaker performance on both procedural and conceptual counting tasks. These findings might be a confirmation of the conclusions of Rittle-Johnson, Siegler and Wagner (2001) who postulated that the development of procedural and conceptual knowledge may be iterative. At any rate, the results imply that it is not only important to assess how accurately young children can count (procedural knowledge) but also how they master the counting principles of Gallistel and Gelman (1992), an aspect of the conceptual counting knowledge. Our dataset confirms the hypothesis that both forms of counting knowledge are distinct and are significant prospective predictors of mathematical proficiency, and therefore should be assessed separately. The findings that both logical abilities and counting knowledge are important in the prediction of mathematical abilities are in line with the theory of Dumont (1994). In his work he maintained that both the Piagetian and neo-Piagetian insights should be integrated into one model on the development of mathematical abilities. Based on our findings, we stress the importance of this integration, but we strongly believe that additional components should be included. First of all, we found evidence for the importance of both procedural and conceptual counting knowledge; theoretical models on the development of mathematical abilities should include both components.

Furthermore, it has recently been suggested that representation of number size is also involved in numerical competence (Jordan, Kaplan, Olah, & Locuniak, 2006). Although in our first study (presented in the pilot study), we could not replicate the findings of Durand, Hulme, Larkin and Snowling (2005) that magnitude comparison was an important predictor of variation in mathematical abilities. We found evidence that low achieving children tended to have lower scores on magnitude comparison tasks than typically achieving children. These findings are in line with several other important research studies in this domain.

Children with mathematical disabilities have been found to have problems with magnitude comparison tasks (Desoete et al., 2011; Desoete & Grégoire, 2007; Landerl, Bevan, & Butterworth, 2004; Stock et al., 2010), and children who had poor mathematical abilities in first grade have been found to have below-average skills in comparing dot sets in kindergarten (Desoete et al., 2011; Desoete & Grégoire, 2007; Stock et al., 2009a;b;c). Furthermore, the analyses in study 5 showed that performances on magnitude comparison tasks were the only preparatory mathematical abilities that differentiated between low achieving children and children with mathematical disabilities. It was stressed that magnitude comparison performances served as the most important kindergarten marker for the detection of mathematical disabilities in second grade.

These findings stress the need for a comprehensive theoretical model on the development of mathematical abilities that includes seriation and classification as logical abilities, both procedural and conceptual counting knowledge, and magnitude comparison. This model could not only promote insight into the development of mathematical abilities, it could also serve as a framework for a better understanding of the development of mathematical disabilities. However, the studies presented have not consistently pointed out one specific predictor or a recurrent combination of predictors. This is in line with the findings of Gersten and colleagues (2005), who found that children with mathematical disabilities do not have stable profiles, and this further strengthens the hypothesis that mathematical performances can shift over time. This makes it clear that it is not good practice to base a diagnosis on a one-time assessment and that it is not advisable to look for a single deficient mathematical ability. These conclusions indicate that it is important to build models that include several markers for mathematical development and then investigate the interactions between those components. Furthermore, it will be important to follow the performances of individual children over time.

7.2.3. Prediciting Later Mathematical Abilities

What can we expect from a theoretical model on mathematical development that integrates these different preparatory mathematical abilities? Can this kind of framework explain large parts of the variance in children's mathematical abilities? The results of our first study on a small sample (as presented in the pilot study) were very promising. Based on the kindergarten performances on these preparatory mathematical abilities, about half of the variance in mathematical reasoning and about one-third of the variance in numerical facility in first grade could be predicted. These figures attributed an enormous predictive value to the preparatory mathematical abilities, and the results were very promising for the use of assessment batteries that include these preparatory mathematical abilities. Unfortunately, our studies on larger samples and with longitudinal data could not offer a confirmation of these first findings. Only smaller percentages of variances in mathematical reasoning and numerical facility could be explained in the three-year longitudinal study (described in study 4). However, rather moderate proportions of performances on mathematical reasoning tasks could be explained by the preparatory mathematical abilities, ranging from 19 percent in the beginning of first grade to 26 percent at the end of first grade, and even increasing to 36 percent in the beginning of second grade. Yet, the percentage of explained variance in mathematical reasoning scores decreased to 11 percent at the end of second grade. These data revealed that, over time, there are many other factors (e.g., school context, see further) that also influence children's mathematical performances (see also Van Steenbrugge, Valcke, & Desoete, 2010) . Concerning the prediction of numerical facility scores, only about 16 percent of the variance of these scores at the beginning of first grade could be explained by the kindergarten markers. This is only about half of the proportion that was found in the first study, presented in the pilot study. Furthermore, it was clear that the role of kindergarten preparatory mathematical abilities in the prediction of numerical facility further decreased on the long term, explaining only 6 percent of the variance in numerical facility at the end of second grade. No clear explanations for these differences can be given. Besides the large differences in sample size, the main difference between the pilot study and the longitudinal study is the fact that magnitude comparison was not included as a kindergarten predictor in the longitudinal study. However, since no significant differences on magnitude comparison tasks between the low achieving and at least moderately achieving children were found, we propose that inclusion of this factor cannot account for the large differences in variances.

7.2.4. Educational Influences

We proposed a model for the mathematical development that included seriation, classification, procedural and conceptual counting knowledge and magnitude comparison.

However, it is clear that a large part of the variance in mathematical abilities still cannot be explained. Based on the study that was presented in study 3, we can add another important factor to our theory. It was found that about one-fifth of the variance in mathematical reasoning and a similar proportion of numerical facility that could be attributed to factors that were associated with school context. The results are in line with the findings of earlier research in Flanders primary (Ministerie van de Vlaamse Gemeenschap, 2004) and secondary (Opdenakker & Van Damme, 2006) schools, which found that between 15 and 20 percent of variance in mathematical achievement scores could be attributed to school variance.

The results outline that there are important differences between schools, so theories on the development of mathematical abilities should not only take into account the individual processes of children, but should also involve the context in which children grow up.

7.2.5. Children at Risk for the Development of Mathematical Disabilities

Across the different studies, we looked to see whether we could predict if children were typical or low achieving in mathematics based on the kindergarten preparatory mathematical abilities. Overall, relatively good categorizations of children's mathematical performances could be made. When predicting performance on numeric abilities in kindergarten, 94 percent of the children were classified correctly, whereas it was possible to classify correctly the mathematical performance of 87 percent of first and 73 percent of second graders respectively. The longer the follow-up period, the weaker the classification results, but assessment of preparatory mathematical abilities in kindergarten seemed to have quite good predictive value for the categorization of mathematical abilities, even two years later.

Still, some important deficiencies have to be illustrated. Whereas all the classification results showed that, based on the preparatory mathematical abilities, 96 percent of the children were classified correctly as typically or at least moderately achieving in mathematics, it was far more difficult to detect the low achieving children or children with mathematical disabilities. It was found that 77 percent of low achieving kindergartners and 67 percent of low achieving first graders could be detected. In the long term, only 29 percent of children with mathematical disabilities in second grade could be flagged and only 5 percent of low achieving children were classified as such. Generally, these results showed that the detection of children with weak mathematical abilities based on preparatory abilities showed good specificity but low sensitivity. Based on our dataset, it seems to be easier to screen the children who are not at risk than to detect the at-risk children based on their preparatory abilities. Geary, Bailey and Hoard (2009) added a speed factor to this assessment and revealed that, based on children's performance in first grade, two out of three children could be identified as having mathematical disabilities at the end of third grade. These results are much better than the classification results we obtained; perhaps these differences have to do with the older age at which the markers were assessed, or the inclusion of the speed factor could have been responsible for the better classification results obtained.

7.2.6. Criteria in Defining Children with Mathematical Disabilities

Some conclusions have to be drawn on the definition of children with mathematical disabilities. Most of the time the selection of children with mathematical abilities for research was based on a distribution of achievement scores; however, across studies, children were selected as having mathematical disabilities based on cut-offs ranging from percentile 3 to as high as percentile 45 (American Psychiatric Association, 2000; Klauer, 1992; Kosc, 1974; Mazzocco, 2001). In this book and in agreement with the recent research of Murphy, Mazzocco, Hanich and Early (2007), children were consistently classified as low achieving when they performed less than or equal to the 10th percentile on the mathematical tests. This cut-off was chosen in line with the current Belgian clinical criterion for mathematical disabilities and the international criterion for reading disabilities (De Clerck et al., 2008; Desoete et al., 2010; Desoete, Ghesquière, Walgraeve, & Thomassen, 2006). One of the purposes of study 5 was to compare the profile of (clinical) children who were selected based on this restrictive criterion with the profile of children who were achieving below the 25th percentile (in study 5, children were defined as having mathematical disabilities and as low achieving children respectively). In order to be sure of the persistence of the disabilities, children were selected based on their scores in two consecutive years. The implementation of such a resistance criterion is important because it was found that performance in children meeting the criteria for mathematical disabilities at one point in time could not be generalized to children who successively meet criteria year after year (Mazzocco, 2001; Murphy et al., 2007; Stock et al., 2010b;c).

The results showed that different conclusions could be drawn when using restrictive or lenient criteria. The conclusions demonstrated that children selected with restrictive criteria and children selected with lenient criteria showed different profiles in kindergarten, with the former having more disturbed mathematical abilities than the latter. This supports the fact that results of low achievers cannot automatically be generalized to children with mathematical disabilities, implying major consequences for the selection of samples in further research. It is hypothesised that children with mathematical disabilities show qualitatively different profiles than children who are low achieving in mathematics, and this hypothesis is confirmed by the recent findings of Mazzocco, Devlin, and McKenney (2008) in older children. They also found that children with mathematical disabilities showed qualitatively different profiles in fact retrieval performances when compared to typically achieving children, whereas the differences between low achieving and typically achieving children were of a quantitative nature. However, most scientific studies still use a more lenient criterion, so we have to be careful with research conclusions on these kinds of samples. The use of divergent selection criteria in the recruitment of research samples of children with mathematical disabilities may have conflated children with severe and mild forms of mathematical disabilities (Geary, Hoard, Byrd-Craven, Nugent, & Numtee, 2007). This may have dispelled a clear and accurate idea of the nature of the disability; complicating identification, diagnosis, treatment and remediation of children with mathematical disabilities (Hamill, 1990).

7.2.7. The Role of Intelligence

The analyses in study 4 showed that intelligence had a significant contribution in the prediction of mathematical abilities in first and second grade, but this was very specific to the prediction of mathematical reasoning and not for the prediction of fact retrieval. These results indicate that intelligence can be seen as an important candidate when looking for useful predictors. This is in agreement with the results of Nunes and colleagues (2006), who found that general cognitive abilities made a significant contribution to the prediction of children's mathematical abilities, even after controlling for logical thinking abilities and working memory. Although intelligence proved to explain significant proportions of the variation in mathematical abilities, we have evidence that within the age range of our dataset and with these specific children it is not a good enough marker for the detection of children who are at risk for the development of mathematical disabilities. In the longitudinal study (presented in study 5), it was shown that, in our dataset, intellectual ability had no added value for the classification of children as having mathematical disabilities, low achieving or typically achieving. This indicates that the problems children with mathematical disabilities in our study encounter cannot be reduced to lower intellectual abilities. Besides, no significant differences in the intellectual capacities between the three groups were found. In conclusion, intellectual abilities play a role in the general development of mathematical abilities, but it is not correct to state that children with low intellectual abilities are per definition at risk for the development of mathematical disabilities, or vice versa that above-average intelligence children cannot be at risk for mathematical disabilities. This is in line with Mazzocco and Myers (2003) and Siegel (1989) who pointed

General Discussion 63

out that there is no logical or empirical ground for involving IQ measurements in the detection of learning disabilities because no differences in the basic cognitive processes can be found among children of different IQ levels.

7.2.8. Limitations and Future Challenges

There are some general limitations that are of concern for the study in its totality. The main limitation is a limitation that is inherent in doing research: the studies in this project overlooked other possible powerful predictors for the development of mathematical (dis)abilities that were not taken into account. In the next section we will address the importance of other preparatory mathematical abilities and subitizing; the role of language in the development of mathematical abilities; the underlying cognitive factors and other influencing factors like context variables.

First of all, some other preparatory (mathematical) abilities were not included in the studies. Only seriation, classification and conservation were included as logical thinking abilities; for the moment we did not focus on the role of inclusion, correspondence and additive composition. Piaget and Szeminska (1941) described inclusion as the highest form of classification. Based on their understanding of seriation and classification, children learn how to make hierarchical classifications when they learn that numbers are series that contain each other. On the other hand, correspondence has only implicitly been mentioned as a preparatory logical thinking ability that is strongly related to conservation (Ruijssenaars, 1992).

Furthermore, it has been found that the understanding of correspondence can be reduced to a component of counting since counting can be seen as the attribution of a label (the counting word) to the counted objects (Kingma, 1981; Koster, 1975). Finally, the command of additive composition holds that children comprehend that any number can be expressed as the sum of two other numbers (or decomposed into two other numbers). This ability is based on children's understanding of conservation; once children know that the number of objects in a collection only changes when one or more objects are added or removed, children understand that quantities can be divided into different components without changing the total number. Since the understanding of seriation, classification and conservation forms the foundation for the development of an understanding of the inclusion principle, correspondence and additive composition, these last components were not taken into account in the current studies.

Secondly, many researchers are currently addressing subitizing as a possible core deficit that is (partly) responsible for the development of mathematical (dis)abilities (Butterworth, 2005; Ceulemans et al., 2011; Dehaene, 1992; De Smedt & Gilmore, 2011; Gersten et al., 2005; Holloway & Ansari, 2008; Landerl et al., 2004). Since subitizing abilities are often studied in very young children (even in one-week-old infants or in four-month-olds) we did not include subitizing measures in this follow-up study starting with children in the last kindergarten class (Antell & Keating, 1983; Bermejo, Morales, & Garcia deOsuna, 2004; Starkey & Cooper, 1980). However, additional research on subitizing as a potential marker in even younger children might be interesting. Magnitude comparison tasks were included in this study. Magnitude comparison can be seen as an ability that further builds on the core subitizing abilities of children (Bermejo et al., 2004). Since it has been found that magnitude comparison is an important predictor of variations in mathematical abilities (Durand et al., 2005), we thought it was more appropriate to include this kind of task for children of these ages.

The development of mathematical (dis)abilities has also been related to the development of language. It has been found that about one-tenth of children with mathematical disabilities in elementary school had some kind of language disorder in kindergarten (Desoete, 2008a; Shalev et al., 2001). Many neurocognitive models on mathematical abilities have included language as a contributing factor in mathematical development. However, striking differences exist between the models on numerical cognition concerning the relationship between semantic information and the input and output. Some models claim that all input (e.g., the verbal numeral 'five' and nonverbal Arabic digit '5') goes through the semantic system, involving an abstract internal representation (e.g., McCloskey, 1992; Gallistel & Gelman, 1992). From that point of view, some forms of mathematical disabilities can also be seen as difficulties with the linguistic translation of operations on quantities (Van Borsel, 1998). However, evidence for non-semantic number naming has been reported (Cipolotti & Butterworth, 1995; Cohen & Dehaene, 1991; Deloche & Seron, 1987). In addition, Dehaene (1992) postulated three interconnected number systems: an analogue magnitude (semantic) representation for number comparison and approximate calculation, a visual system for parity judgments and multidigit operations and an auditory-verbal word frame making use of general language modules and having access to stored mathematical facts. Notwithstanding this evidence, no linguistic factors have been added in the current analyses in order to avoid complication of the research questions and the analyses. However, these kinds of measures have been included in the follow-up project and will be analysed in future research. In line with the current Belgian approach to mathematical disabilities, this study approached the development of mathematical (dis)abilities in a descriptive way (Desoete et al., 2010).

Besides the urge to look for powerful descriptive markers, it would be interesting to look for the underlying cognitive processes that could explain the development of mathematical (dis)abilities. Several authors stressed the importance of metacognition (Desoete, 2007b; 2009a & b; Desoete & Veenman, 2006a, 2006b; Vanderswalmen, Vrijders, & Desoete, 2010), executive functions (e.g., Mazzocco & Kover, 2007; Van der Sluis, de Jong, & van der Leij, 2007), attention (Marzocchi, Lucangeli, De Meo, Fini, & Cornoldi, 2002) and working memory (e.g., Geary & Widaman, 1992; Ketelsen & Welsh, 2010; Nunes et al., 2006; Passolunghi, Mammarella, & Altoe, 2008; Ricken & Fritz, 2006) in the development of mathematical (dis)abilities. Studies on the central executive component of working memory have provided insight into the deficits of children with mathematical disabilities (Barrouillet, Fayol, & Lathuliére, 1997; Geary et al., 2007; Geary, Hamson, & Hoard, 2000), but it will be necessary to focus on these competencies before the start of formal schooling in order to obtain insight that can contribute to the early identification of children with mathematical disabilities (Geary et al., 2009; Gersten et al., 2005). In this study we consciously aimed to approach the development of mathematical (dis)abilities in a descriptive way.

Finally, it would be clarifying to include both descriptive preparatory mathematical abilities and measures of underlying cognitive processes in the same study in order to have a thorough view of the relations and interactions between these components. Furthermore, it has been found that normal age-related changes in basic cognitive systems, such as working memory, may interact with early schooling (Geary, 2000). This interaction can result in a solid base for the further development of proficient mathematical abilities, whereas the combination with poor early schooling may cause the onset of mathematical disabilities.

These limitations indicate that only part of the picture was investigated, so the conclusions have to be interpreted with care. Besides the addition of the factors mentioned in further research projects, we see two main challenges for future research. First of all, it is necessary that more attention be given to the development of an empirically based, unifying model that explains the development of mathematical abilities. These models should not only focus on the importance of preparatory abilities, but also investigate the role of underlying and associated cognitive and attentional processes, the role of context measures and educational influences. If fundamental research could provide this kind of comprehensive model, this could function as a framework for further research on the development of mathematical disabilities. The second, and perhaps most important, challenge for the future is to accommodate the need for intervention studies (Gersten et al., 2005). Early intervention can remediate difficulties and alter children's mathematical development (Fuchs & Fuchs, 2001), but if we really want to screen children on their early mathematical abilities in order to prevent the development of mathematical disabilities, it will be important to focus on assessments that are directly related to instruction. Only responses to instruction studies can sufficiently serve that goal (Fletcher, Coulter, Reschly, & Vaughn, 2004).

7.2.9. Implications

Based on the conclusions of these studies, some important implications can be drawn. We distinguish implications that are of concern for researchers and implications for clinical practice.

First of all, a comprehensive theoretical model is needed that describes the development of mathematical abilities. In the last decade, several models of adult mathematical problem solving have been proposed, based on normal adults or on patient data (e.g., Cipolotti, 1995; McCloskey, 1992). However, there still seems to be disagreement on several issues, and the development of the children's mathematical abilities has been studied within different theoretical frameworks. Developmental models often focus on specific aspects or sub-skills, such as counting (Gallistel & Gelman, 1992), calculation (Levine, Jordan, & Huttenlocher, 1992) or constructing two-digit numbers (e.g., Fuson, Richards, & Briars, 1982; Fuson, Wearne, Hiebert, Murray, Human, Olivier, Carpenter, & Fennema, 1997). Most of the time, preparatory abilities were not included in these models or research is focused only on Piagetian or only on neo-Piagetian skills. We propose to integrate logical abilities such as seriation and classification in a model that also includes procedural and conceptual counting knowledge. Dumont (1994) integrated logical abilities with counting, but he did not differentiate between procedural counting knowledge and conceptual counting knowledge. In addition, we found evidence that it might be interesting to include magnitude comparison as precursors for the development of representation of number size when focusing on mathematical disabilities. Moreover, the findings of the studies further implicate that context variables should also be included. Furthermore, researchers should be aware that a large part of the variance in mathematical abilities cannot yet been explained. We defend a model that includes both descriptive mathematical abilities and underlying cognitive factors, taking into account the larger context. However, additional research is needed to build such a model.

Secondly, researchers should be careful when composing clinical samples of children with mathematical disabilities. The current use of divergent and frequently lenient selection criteria in the recruitment of research samples of children with mathematical disabilities has conflated children with severe and mild forms of mathematical disabilities, dispelling a clear and accurate idea of the nature of the disability. It has been shown in study 5 that different conclusions can be drawn when other selection criteria for clinical samples are used. Children selected with restrictive criteria and children selected with lenient criteria showed different mathematical profiles in kindergarten, with the former having more disturbed mathematical abilities than the latter. This supports the fact that results of studies on low achievers cannot automatically be generalized to children with mathematical disabilities. Since the problems of identification of mathematical disabilities can be reduced by increasing specificity and the use of strict identification criteria (Scruggs & Mastropieri, 2002), it is important to not only include low achieving children but also children who correspond to the restrictive clinical selection criteria of mathematical disability. Adopting the selection criteria in research samples to the criteria used in clinical practice enables a more accurate application of research findings to clinical practice. Furthermore, in order to be sure of the persistence of the disabilities, the implementation of a RTI (lack of response to instruction) or resistance criterion is important because it has been found that performance in children meeting criteria for mathematical disabilities at one point in time could not be generalized to children who successively meet criteria year after year (Mazzocco, 2001; Murphy et al., 2007).

Based on the findings of these studies, we can also draw some implications for practitioners who work with children with mathematical disabilities. Clinicians who are involved in the assessment and remediation of children with mathematical disabilities are encouraged to use assessment batteries that include logical thinking abilities like seriation and classification. Moreover, it was found that it is not only important to assess how accurately young children can count (procedural knowledge), but also the extent to which they understand the underlying counting principles (conceptual counting knowledge). Finally, we found evidence for the inclusion of magnitude comparison tasks in assessment batteries that intend to detect children at risk for the development of mathematical disabilities. It has even been found that performances on magnitude comparison tasks were the only preparatory mathematical ability that differentiated between low achieving children and children with mathematical disabilities. The studies in this research investigation have not consistently pointed out one specific predictor or a recurrent combination of predictors. This further strengthens the hypothesis that mathematical performances can shift over time, implying that it is not good practice to base a diagnosis on a one-time assessment, and that it might be an oversimplification to look for a single deficient mathematical ability. It is recommended that not only the individual preparatory mathematical abilities be assessed, but rather a set of markers when predictions of later mathematical abilities want to be made. Furthermore, since it was far more difficult to detect the low achieving children or children with mathematical disabilities compared to typically achieving children, the use of preparatory abilities as markers can only serve as a rough and global screening of children with mathematical disabilities beside a more global anamnesis. This implies that it will be important to follow the performances of the individual at-risk children over time.

Besides, although intellectual abilities have been found to play a role in the development of mathematical abilities, we found in our specific sample of children and within this age range no significant differences in the intellectual capacities between the children with mathematical disabilities, low achieving children and typically achieving children. We are convinced that intellectual abilities play a role in the general development of mathematical abilities, but children with low intellectual abilities are not per definition at risk for the development of mathematical disabilities. The assessment of intellectual abilities can be an important indicator for the adaptation of remediation programs to the individual child. Yet, based on the data in this book and in line with Mazzocco and Myers (2003) and Siegel (1989), we found no evidence that the inclusion of intelligence in the assessment of mathematical disabilities has some value added to the regular screening batteries for the detection of mathematical disabilities.

Finally, evidence was found that, even before the start of formal schooling, different groups of typically or low achieving children could be outlined. Children have a great variety of preparatory abilities when they enter elementary school. Teachers should be aware of these important differences in mathematical skills children bring with them when entering formal schooling. Furthermore, important influences have been attributed to the school context; research has to investigate further which factors in this context play an important role. This could enable teachers to adapt their teaching practice so children who are at risk for the development of mathematical disabilities could be remediated as soon as possible.

CONCLUSIONS

These studies investigated whether early markers for the mathematical development could be recognised. We investigated the role of preparatory mathematical abilities in the prediction of later mathematical performances in a large group of children with a broad range of mathematical abilities. It was found that there were important differences in the mathematical skills of children when they started formal schooling, and this was even the case for basic mathematical abilities that supposedly require no formal schooling. It was found that kindergartners' performance on seriation, classification, procedural counting, conceptual counting and magnitude comparison tasks could serve as powerful predictors for later mathematical abilities. Based on these markers, significant proportions of later mathematical abilities could be explained, and this set of preparatory mathematical abilities were shown to have good predictive value for the categorization of children's later mathematical performances. However, it is important to take into account the influence of the school context, and researchers have to look further for explanations for the variance in mathematical abilities that remains unexplained. It was found that researchers have to be careful when selecting clinical samples since different conclusions could be drawn when using restrictive or lenient criteria.

We further stressed the need for a comprehensive theoretical model that integrates the Piagetian theory on logical abilities and the neo-Piagetian insights on the development of counting knowledge, complemented with recent findings on the importance of representation of number size. Finally, it is recommended that we should not try to assess one specific preparatory ability, but rather look for a set of markers when predictions of later mathematical ability needs to be made.

REFERENCES

American Psychiatric Association (2000). *Diagnostic and statistical manual of mental disorders. Fourth edition, Text Revision.* Washington, DC: Author.

Antell, S., & Keating, D.P. (1983). Perception of numerical invariance in neonates. *Child Development, 54*, 695-701.

Arlin, P. K. (1981). Piagetian Tasks as Predictors of Reading and Math Readiness in Grades-K-1. Journal of Educational Psychology, 73, 712-721.

Aunola, K., Leskinen, E., Lerkkanen, M.-K., & Nurmi, J.-E. (2004). Developmental Dynamics of Math Performance from Preschool to Grade 2. *Journal of Educational Psychology, 96,* 699-713.

Badian, N. A. (1983). Aritmetic and nonverbal learning. In Myklebust, H. R. (Ed). Progress in learning disabilities, vol 5 (pp 235-264). New York: Grune and Stratton.

Barbaresi, W. J., Katusic, S. C., Colligan, R. C., Waever, A. L., & Jacobsen, S. J. (2005). Math learning disorder: Incidence in a population-based birth cohort, 1976-82, Rochester, Minn. Ambulatory Pediatrics, 5, 281-289.

Baroody, A. J. (1992). Remedying common counting difficulties. In J. Bideaud, C. Meljac, & J.-P. Fischer (Eds), Pathways to number. Children's developing numerical abilities (307-324). Hillsdale, NJ: Erlbaum.

Barrouillet, P., Fayol, M., & Lathuliere, E. (1997). Selecting between competitors in multiplication tasks: An explanation of the errors produced by adolescents with learning difficulties. *International Journal of Behavioral Development, 21,* 253-275.

Barrouillet, P., & Lepine, R. (2005). Working memory and children's use of retrieval to solve addition problems. *Journal of Experimental Child Psychology, 91,* 183-204.

Baudonck, M., Debusschere, A., Dewulf, B., Samyn, F., Vercaemst, V., & Desoete, A. (2006). De Kortrijkse Rekentest Revision KRT-R. [The Kortrijk Arithmetic Test Revision KRT-R]. Kortrijk: CAR Overleie

Bermejo, V., Morales, S., & Garcia de Osuna, J. (2004). Supporting children's development of cardinality understanding. *Learning and Instruction, 14,* 381- 98.

Blöte, A. W., Lieffering, L. M., & Ouwehand, K. (2006). The development of manyto-one counting in 4-year-old children. *Cognitive Development, 21,* 332-348.

Briars, D., & Siegler, R. S. (1984). A featural analysis of children's counting. *Developmental Psychology, 20,* 607-618.

Burbaud, P., Degreze, P., Lafon, P., Franconi, J. M., Bouligand, B., Bioulac, B., Caille, J. M., & Allard, M. (1995). Lateralisation of prefrontal activation during internal mental calculation : a functional magnetic resonance imaging study. *Journal of Neurophysiology, 74,* 2194-2200.

Briars, D., & Siegler, R. S. (1984). A featural analysis of children's counting. *Developmental Psychology, 20,* 607-618.

Butterworth, B. (2004). The development of arithmetical abilities. *Journal of Child Psychology and Psychiatry, 46,* 3-18.

Butterworth, B. (2005). The development of arithmetical abilities. *Journal of Child Psychology and Psychiatry, 46,* 3-18.

Cahan, S., Greenbaum, C., Artman, L., Deluya, N., & Gappel-Gilon, Y. (2008). The differential effects of age and first grade schooling on the development of infralogical and logico-mathematical concrete operations. *Cognitive Development, 23,* 258-277.

References 75

Campbell, J. I. D., & Clark, J. M. (1988). An encoding complex view of cognitive number processing: comment on McCloskey, Sokol and Goodman (1986). *Journal of Experimental Psychology: General, 117,* 204-214.

Ceulemans, A., Desoete, A., Roeyers, H. (april 2010). Individual Differences in number discrimination in infants. Paper IInd European Conference on Dyslexia. KHBO: Brugges.

Ceulemans, A., Desoete, A., Hoppenbrouwers, K., & Van Leeuwen, K. (2011). Exploring number discrimination abilities from infancy to toddlerhood. Paper at the third expert meeting for mathematic researchers from the Benelux. 11th February. Ghent University.

Cohen, L., & Dehaene, S. (1991). Neglect dyslexia for numbers? A case report.*Cognitive Neuropsychology, 8,* 39-58.

Cornoldi, C., & Lucangeli, D. (2004). Arithmetic Education and Learning Disabilities in Italy. *Journal of Learning Disabilities, 37,* 42-49.

Cipolotti, L. (1995). Multiple routes for reading words, why not numbers? Evidence from a case of Arabic numeral dyslexia. *Cognitive Neuropsychology, 12,* 313-362.

Cipolotti, L. & Butterworth, B. (1995). Toward a multiroute model of number processing: Impaired number transcoding with preserved calculation skills. *Journal of Experimental Psychology: General, 124,* 375-390.

Colom, R., & Flores-Mendoza, C., E. (2007). Intelligence predicts scholastic achievement irrespective of SES factors: Evidence from Brazil. *Intelligence, 35,* 243-251.

De Clerck, D., Lahou, S., Marrannes, J., Milleville, M., Van Hul, K., & Vonckx, C. (2008). *Traject bij vermoeden van dyscalculia [Route when suspecting dyscalculia].* Brussel: VCLB.

Dehaene, S. (1992).Varieties of numerical abilities. *Cognition, 44,* 1-42.

Dehaene, S., & Cohen, L. (1991). Two mental calculation systems: A case study of severe acalculia with preserved approximation. *Neuropsychologia, 29,* 1045-1074.

Dehaene, S., Spelke, E., Pinel, P., Stanescu, R., & Tsivkin, S. (1999). Sources of mathematical thinking: behavioral and brain-imaging evidence. *Science, 284,* 970-973.

Dehaene, S., Tzourio, N., Frak, V. Raynaud, L., Cohen, L., Mehler, J., & Mazoyer, B. (1996). Cerebral activations during number multiplication and comparison: A PET study. *Neuropsychologia, 29,* 1097-1106.

Deloche, G., & Seron, X. (1987). Numerical transcoding: A general production model. In G. Deloche & X. Seron (Eds.), *Mathematical Disabilities: A Cognitive Neuropsychological Perspective* (pp. 137-170). Hillsdale, NJ: Erlbaum.

Denburg, N. L., & Tranel, D. (2003). Acaluclia and Disturbances of the Body Schema. In Heilman, K. M., & Valentstein, E. (Eds). *Clinical Neuropsychology, fourth edition* (pp 161-184). Oxford: University Press.

De Smedt, B., & Gilmore, C.K. (2011). Defective number module or impaired acces? Numerical magnitude processing in first graders with mathematical difficulties. *Journal of Experimental Child Psychology, 108,* 278-292.

Desoete, A. (2007a). *Students with mathematical disabilities in Belgium: from definition, classification and assessment to STICORDI devices.* (pp. 181-222). In T.E. Scruggs & M.A. Mastropieri (Eds.), Advances in Learning and Behavioral Disabilities, Vol. 20. International Perspectives Amsterdam & Oxford: Elsevier Press.

Desoete, A. (2007b). Evaluating and improving the mathematics teaching-learning process through metacognition? *Electronic Journal of Research in Educational Psychology,* 5 (3), 705-730.

Desoete, A. (2008a). Co-morbidity in mathematical learning disabilities: Rule or exception? *The Open rehabilitation Journal, 1,* 15-26.

Desoete, A. (2008b). Do birth order, family size and gender affect arithmetic achievement in elementary school? *Electronic Journal of Research in Educational Psychology, 6* (1), 135-156.

Desoete, A. (2009a). Mathematics and metacognition in adolescents and adults with learning disabilities. *International Electronic Journal of Elementary Eduction, 2* (1), 82-100.

References 77

Desoete, A. (2009b). Metacognitive prediction and evaluation skills and mathematical learning in third-grade students. *Educations Research and Evaluation, 15*, 435-446.

Desoete, A. (2010). Expert commentary: *Directions and Misdirections in Mathematical Learning Disability Studies.* In Spencer B. Thompson (Ed.). Kindergartens: Programs, Functions and Outcomes (pp 215-218). Nova Science Publishers (NY, USA).

Desoete, A., Ceulemans, A., De Weerdt, F., & Pieters, S. (2011). Can we predict mathematical learning disabilities from symbolic and non-symbolic comparison tasks in kindergarten? Findings from a longitudinal study. *British Journal of Educational Psychology*, in press.

Desoete, A., Ceulemans, A., Roeyers, H., & Huylebroeck, A. (2009).Subitzing or counting as possible screening variables for learning disabilities in mathematics education or learning. *Educational Research Review, 4,* 55-66.

Desoete, A., Ghesquière, P., De Smedt, B., Andries, C., Van den Broeck, W., & Ruijssenaars, W. (2010). Dyscalculie: standpunt van onderzoekers in Vlaanderen en Nederland. *[Dyscalculia: Point of view of researchers in Flanders and in the Netherlands] Logopedie, 23* (4), 4-9.

Desoete, A., Ghesquière, P., Walgraeve, T., & Thomassen, J. (2006). Dyscalculie: stand van zaken in Vlaanderen [Dyscalculia: The state of affairs in Flanders]. In M. Dolk & M. van Groenestijn (Ed.), *Dyscalculie in discussie. Op weg naar consensus [Dyscalculia in discussion. Towards a consensus]* (pp. 51-63). Assen: Van Gorcum.

Desoete, A., & Grégoire, J. (2007). Numerical competence in young children and in children with mathematics learning disabilities. *Learning and Individual Differences, 16,* 351-367.

Desoete, A., & Ozsoy, G. (2009). Introduction: Metacognition, more than the lognes monser? International Electronic Journal of Elementary Education (IEJEE), 2 (1), 2-6.

Desoete, A., & Stock, P. (2010). Can we predict mathematical disabilities from abilities in kindergarten. In Spencer B. Thompson (Ed.). Kindergartens: Programs, Functions and Outcomes (pp 1-49). Nova Science Publishers (NY, USA).

Desoete, A., Stock, P., Schepens, A., Baeyens, D., & Roeyers, H. (2009). Classification, seriation, and counting in Grades 1, 2 , and 3 as two year longitudinal predictors for low achieving in numerical facility and arithmetical achievement, *Journal of Psychoeducational Assessment*, 27, 252-264.

Desoete, A., Roeyers, H., & De Clercq, A. (2004). Children with mathematics learning disabilities in Belgium. *Journal of Learning Disabilities, 37,* 50-61.

Desoete, A., & Veenman, M. (2006a). Metacognition in mathematics: Critical issues on nature, theory, assessment and treatment. In A. Desoete & M. Veenman (Eds), Metacognition in mathematics education (pp. 1-10). NOVA: New York

Desoete, A, & Roeyers, H. (2006b). Current issues in the assessent and training of metacognition related to mathematical problem solving. In Mitel, Alea V. (Ed.) *Focus on Educational Psychology* (pp. 251-275). Hauppauge NY: Nova Science Publishers.

De Vos, T. (1992). *TTR. Tempotest rekenen [Arithmetic number fact test].* Lisse: Swets & Zeitlinger.

Dowker, A.D. (2001). Numeracy recovery: A pilot scheme for early intervention with young children with numeracy difficulties. *Support for Learning, 16*, 6-10.

Dowker, A. (2004). *What works for children with mathematical difficulties. Research Report No 554.*University of Oxford: UK.

Dowker, A. (2005). *Individual Differences in Arithmetic. Implications for Psychology, Neuroscience and Education.* New York: Psychology Press.

Dumont, J.J. (1994). *Leerstoornissen I. Theorie en model (nieuwe uitgave) [Learning disabilities I. Theory and model (new edition)].* Rotterdam: Lemniscaat.

Duncan, G. J., Dowsett, C. J., Claessens, A., Magnuson, K., Huston, A. C., Klebanov, P., Pagani, L. S., Feinstein, L., Egel, M., Brooks-Gunn, J., Sexton, H., Duckworth, K., & Japel, C. (2007). School Readiness and Later Achievement. *Developmental Psychology, 43,* 1428-1446.

References

Durand, M., Hulme, C., Larkin, R., & Snowling, M. (2005). The cognitive foundations of reading and arithmetic skills in 7- to 10-year olds. *Journal of Experimental Child Psychology, 91,* 113-136.

Fisk, J. L., & Rourke, B. P. (1979). Identification of subtypes of learning-disabled children at three age levels: A neuropsychological, multivariate approach. *Journal of Clinical Neuropsychology, 1,* 289-310.

Fletcher, J. M., Coulter, W. A., Reschly, D. J., & Vaughn, S. (2004). Alternative approaches to the definition and identification of learning disabilities: Some questions and answers. *Annals of Dyslexia, 54,* 304-331.

Frank, A. R. (1989). Counting skills: A foundation for early mathematics. *Arithmetic Teacher, 37,* 14-17.

Freeman, N., H., Antonucci, C., & Lewis, C. (2000). Representation of the cardinality principle: Early conception of error in a counterfactual test. *Cognition, 74,* 71-89.

Frye, D., Braisby, N., Lowe, J., Maroudas, C., & Nicholls, J. (1989). Young children's understanding of counting and cardinality. *Child Development, 60,* 1158-1171.

Fuchs, L. S., & Fuchs, D. (2001). Principles for the prevention and intervention of mathematics difficulties. *Learning Disabilities Research and Practice, 16,* 85-95.

Fuchs, L. S., & Fuchs, D. (2002). Mathematical problem-solving profiles of students with mathematics disabilities with and without comorbid reading disabilities. *Journal of learning disabilities, 35,* 563-573.

Fuson, K. C. (1988). *Children's counting and concepts of number.* New York: Springer Verlag.

Fuson, K.C., Richards, J.,& Briars, D.J. (1982). The acquisition and elaboration of the number word sequence. In C.J. Brainerd (Ed.), *Children's logical and mathematical cognition:Progress in cognitive development research* (pp. 33-92). New York: Springler-Verlag.

Fuson, K.C., Wearne, D., Hiebert, J., Murray, H.G., Human, P.G., Olivier, A.I., Carpenter, T.P.,& Fennema, E. (1997). Children's conceptual structures for multidigit numbers and methods of multidigit addition and subtraction. *Journal of Research in Mathematics Education, 28*, 130-162.

Gadeyne, E., Ghesquière, P., & Onghena, P. (2004). Psychosocial functioning of young children with learning problems. *Journal of Child Psychology and Psychiatry, 45,* 510-521.

Gallistel, C. R., & Gelman, R. (1990). The what and how of counting. *Cognition, 34,* 197- 199.

Gallistel, C., & Gelman, R. (1992). Preverbal and verbal counting and computation. *Cognition, 44,* 43-74.

Geary, D.C. (1994). *Children's Mathematical Development.* Washington, D.C.: American Psychological Association.

Geary, D. C. (2000). From infancy to adulthood: the development of numerical abilities. *Europeran Child & Adolescent Psychiatry, 9,* II/11-II/16.

Geary, D. C. (2004). Mathematics and learning disabilities. *Journal of Learning Disabilities, 37,* 4-15.

Geary, D. C., Bailey, D. H., & Hoard, M. K. (2009). Predicting mathematical achievement and mathematical learning disability with a simple screening tool: The Number Sets Test. *Journal of Psychoeducational Assessment, 27,* 265-279.

Geary, D. C., Bow-Thomas, C. C., & Yao, Y. (1992). Counting knowledge and skill in cognitive addition: A comparison of normal and mathematically disabled children. *Journal of Experimental Child Psychology, 54,* 372-391.

Geary, D. C., & Brown, S. C (1991). Cognitive addition: Strategy choice and speed-of-processing differences in gifted, normal, and mathematically disabled children. *Developmental Psychology*, 27, 398-406.

Geary, D. C., Hamson, C. O., & Hoard, M. K. (2000). Numerical and arithmetical cognition: A longitudinal study of process and concept deficits in children with learning disability. *Journal of Experimental Child Psychology, 77,* 236-263.

Geary, D.C., & Hoard, M.K. (2005). Learning disabilities in arithmetic and mathematics: Theoretical and empirical perspectives. In J.I.D.

References 81

Campbell (Ed.), *Handbook of mathematical cognition* (pp. 253-268). New York: Psychology Press.

Geary, D. C., Hoard, M. K., Byrd-Craven, J., Nugent, L., & Numtee, C. (2007). Cognitive mechanisms underlying achievement deficits in children with mathematical learning disability. *Child Development, 78,* 1343-1359.

Geary, D. C., Hoard, M. K., & Hamson, C. O. (1999). Numerical and Arithmetical Cognition: Patterns of Functions and Deficits in Children at Risk for a Mathematical Disability. *Journal of Experimental Child Psychology, 74,* 213-239.

Geary, D. C., & Widaman, K. F. (1992). Numerical cognition: On the convergence of componential and psychometric models. *Intelligence, 16,* 47-80.

Gelman, R. (1990). First principles organize attention to and learning about relevant data: number and animate-inanimate distinctions as examples. *Cognitive Science, 14,* 79-106.

Gelman, R., & Galistel, C. R. (1978). *The child's understanding of number.* Cambridge, MA: Harvard University Press.

Gelman, R., & Meck, E. (1983). Preschooler's counting: Principles before skill. *Cognition, 13,* 343-359.

Gersten, R., & Chard, D. (1999). Number sense: Rethinking arithmetic instruction for students with mathematical disabilities. *Journal of Special Education, 44,* 18-28.

Gersten, R., Jordan, N. C., & Flojo, J. R. (2005). Early Identification and Intervention for Students with Mathematics Difficulties. *Journal of Learning Disabilities, 38,* 293-304.

Greenham, S. (1999). Learning disabilities and psychosocial adjustment: A critical review. *Child neuropsychology, 5,* 171-196.

Grégoire, J. (2005). Développement logique et compétences arithmétiques. Le modèle piagétien est-il toujours actuel ? In M. Crahay, L. Verschaffel, E. De Corte & J. Grégoire. *Enseignement et apprentissage des mathématiques.* (pp.57-77). Bruxelles : De Boeck.

Grégoire, J., & Desoete, A. (2009). Mathematical Disabilities–An Underestimated Topic?" Journal of *Psychoeducational Assessment*, 27, 171-174.

Gross-Tsur, V., Manor, O. and Shalev, R. S. (1996). Developmental dyscalculia: prevalence and demographic features. *Developmental Medicine and Child Neurology, 38,* 25-33.

Hammill, D. D. (1990). On defining learning disabilities: An emerging consensus. *Journal of learning disabilities, 23,* 74-84.

Hanley, T. V. (2005). Commentary on Early identification and interventions for students with mathematical difficulties: Make sense – Do the math. *Journal of Learning Disabilities, 38,* 346-349.

Hannula, M. M., & Lehtinnen, E. (2005). Spontaneous focussing on numerosity and mathematical skills of young children. *Learning and Instruction, 15,* 237-256.

Haskell, S. H. (2000). The determinants of arithmetic skills in young children: some observations. *European Child & Adolescent Psychiatry, 9,* II/77-II/86.

Hécaen, H., Angelergues, R., & Houillier, S. (1961). Les variétés cliniques des acalculies au cours des lésions rétrorolandiques : Apprroche statistique du problème [The clinical varieties of the acalculies in retrorolandic lesions : A statistical approach to the problem]. *Revue Neurologique, 105,* 85-103.

Holloway, I. D., & Ansari, D. (2008). Mapping numerical magnitudes onto symbols: The numerical distance effect and individual differences in children's mathematics achievement. *Journal of Experimental Child Psychology,* doi:10.1016/j.jecp.2008.04.001

Houssaert, J. (2001). Counting difficulties at Key Stage 2. *Support for Learning, 16,* 11-16.

Johansson, B. S. (2005). Number-word sequence skill and arithmetic performance. *Scandinavian Journal of Psychology, 46,* 157-167.

Jordan, N.C., Hanich, L.B., & Kaplan, B. (2003). A Longitudinal Study of Mathematical Competencies in Children with Specific Mathematics Difficulties Versus Children with Comorbid Mathematics and Reading Difficulties. *Child Development, 74,* 834-850.

References

83

Jordan, N. C., Kaplan, D., Olah, L. N., & Locuniak, M. N. (2006). Numer sense growth in kindergarten: A longitudinal investigation of children at risk for mathematics difficulties. *Child development, 77,* 153-175.

Kamphaus, R. W., Petosky, M. D., & Rowe, E. W. (2000). Current trends in psychological testing of children. *Professional Psychology: Research and Practice, 31,* 155-164.)

Kavale, K. A., & Forness, S. R. (2010). What definitions of learning disability say and don't say. A critical analysis. *Journal of learning disabilities, 33,* 239-256.

Ketelsen, K., & Welsh, M. (2010). Working memory and mental arithmetic: A case for dual central executive resources. Brain and Cognition, 74, 203-209.

Kingma, J. (1981). *De ontwikkeling van quantitatieve en relationele begrippen bij kinderen van 4-12 jaar [The development of quantitative and relational concepts in children of 4-12 years old].* Groningen: Rijksuniversiteit Groningen.

Kingma, J. (1983). Seriation, Correspondence, and Transitivity. *Journal of Educational Psychology, 75,* 763-771.

Kingma, J. (1984). Traditional intelligence, Piagetian Tasks, and Initial Arithmetic in kindergarten and primary-school grade-one. *Journal of Genetic Psychology, 145,* 49-60.

Klauer, K. J. (1992). In Mathematik mehr leistungsschwache Madchen, im Lesen und Rechschreiben mehr leistungsschwache Junden? *Zeitschift fur Entwicklungspsychologie und Padagogische Psychologie, 26,* 48-65.

Knopik, V. S., Alarcón, M., & DeFries, J. C. (1997). Comorbidity of mathematics and reading deficits: Evidence for a genetic etiology. *Behavior Genetics, 27,* 447-453.

Korhonen, T. T. (1991). Neuropsychological stability and prognosis of subgroups of children with learning disabilities. *Journal of learning disabilities, 24,* 48-57.

Kosc, L. (1974). Developmental dyscalculia. *Journal of Learning Disabilities, 7,* 46-59.

Koster, K. B. (1975). *De ontwikkeling van het getalbegrip op de kleuterschool: Een onderzoek naar de effecten van enkele trainingsprogramma's [The development of number in kindergarten: Research on the effects of some training programs].* Groningen: Tjeenk-Willink.

Kronenberger, W. G., & Dunn, D. W. (2003). Learning disorders. *Neurologic Clinics, 21,* 941-952.

Kulak, A. G. (1993). Parrallels between math and reading disability: Common issues and approaches. *Journal of Learning Disabilities, 26,* 666-673.

Landerl, K., Bevan, A., & Butterworth, B. (2004). Developmental dyscalculia and basic numerical capacities: A study of 8-9-year old students. *Cognition, 93,* 99-125.

Laski, E. V., & Siegler, R. S. (2007). Is 27 a big number? Correlational and causal connections among numerical categorization, number line estimation and numerical magnitude comparison. *Child Development, 78,* 1723-1743.

Le Corre, M., Van de Walle, G., Brannon, E. M., & Carey, S. (2006). Revisiting the competence/performance debate in the acquisition of the counting principles. *Cognitive Psychology, 52,* 130-169.

Le Fevre, J.-A., Smith-Chant, B. L., Fast, L., Skwarchuk, S.-L., Sargla, E., Arnup, J. S., Penner-Wilger, M., Bisanz, J., & Kamawar, D. (2006). What counts as knowing? The development of conceptual and procedural knowledge of counting from kindergarten through grade 2. *Journal of Experimental Child Psychology, 93,* 285-303.

Lepola, J., Niemi, P., Kuikka, M., & Hannula, M. M. (2005). Cognitive-linguistic skills and motivation as longitudinal predictors of reading and arithmetic achievement: A follow-up study from kindergarten to grade 2. *International Journal of Educational Research, 43,* 250-271.

Levine, S.C., Jordan, N.C., & Huttenlocher, J. (1992). Development of Calculation Abilities in Young Children. *Journal of Experimental Child Psychology 53,* 72-103

Lewis, C., Hitch, G. J., Walker, P. (1994). The prevalence of specific arithmetic difficulties and specific reading difficulties in 9- to 10-year old boys and girls. *Journal of Child Psychology and Psychiatry, 35,* 283-292.

Light, J. G., & DeFries, J. C. (1995). Comorbidity of reading and mathematics disabilities: Genetic and environmental etiologies. *Journal of Learning Disabilities, 28,* 96-106.

Lourenço, O., & Machado, A. (1996). In Defense of Piaget's Theory: A Reply to 10. Common Criticisms. *Psychological Review, 103,* 143-164.

Marzocchi, G. M., Lucangeli, D., De Meo, T., Fini, F., & Cornoldi, C. (2002). The Disturbing Effect of Irrelevant Information on Arithmetic Problem Solving in Inattentive Children. *Developmental Neuropsychology, 21,* 73-92.

Mazzocco, M. M. M. (2001). Math learning disability and math LD subtypes: Evidence from studies of Turner syndrome, Fragile X syndrome and Neurofibromatosis type 1. *Journal of learning disabilities, 34,* 520-533.

Mazzocco, M. M. M. (2005). Challenges in identifying target skills for math disability screening and intervention. *Journal of Learning Disabilities, 38,* 318-323.

Mazzocco, M. M. M., Devlin, K. T., & McKenney, S. J. (2008). Is it a fact? Timed arithmetic performance of children with mathematical learning disabilities (MLD) varies as a function of how MLD is defined. *Developmental Neuropsychology, 33,* 318-344.

Mazzocco, M. M. M., & Kover, S. T. (2007). A Longitudinal Assessment of Executive Function Skills and Their Association with Math Performance. *Child Neuropsychology, 13,*18-45

Mazzocco, M. M. M., & Myers, G. F. (2003). Complexities in identifying and defining mathematics learning disability in the primary school-age years. *Annals of Dyslexia, 53,* 218-253.

McCloskey, M. (1992). Cognitive mechanisms in numerical processing: Evidence from acquired dyscalculia. *Cognition, 44,* 107-157.

McCloskey, M., Caramazza, A., & Basili, A. (1985). Cognitive mechanisms in number processing and calculation: Evidence from dyscalculia. *Brain and cognition, 4,* 154-182.

McCloskey, M., & Macaruso, P. (1995). Representing and using numerical information. *American Psychologist, 50,* 351-363.

Ministerie van de Vlaamse Gemeenschap (2004). *Eerste peiling wiskunde en lezen in het basisonderwijs [First gauging on arithmetic and reading in elementary education].* Brussels: Boone-Roosens.

Murphy, M. M., Mazzocco, M. M. M., Hanich, L. B., & Early, M. C. (2007). Cognitive characteristics of children with mathematics learning disability (MLD) vary as a function of the cutoff criterion used to define MLD. *Journal of Learning Disabilities, 40,* 458-478.

Mussolin, C., Mejias, S., & Noel, M.P. (2010). Symbolic and nonsymbolic number comparison in children with and without dyscalculia. *Cognition, 115,* 10-25.

Njiokiktjien, C. (2004). *Gedragsneurologie van het kind [Behavior Neurlogy of the child].* Amsterdam: Suyi Publications.

Nunes, T., Bryant, P., Evans, D., Bell, D., Gardner, A., Gardner, A., & Carraher, J. (2006). The contribution of logical reasoning to the learning of mathematics in primary school. *British Journal of Developmental Psychology, 00,* 1-21.

Ofiesch, N. (2006). Response to intervention and the identification of specific learning disabilities: Why we need comprehensive evaluations as part of the process. *Psychology in the Schools, 43,* 883-888.

Ohlsson, S., & Rees, E. (1991). The function of conceptual understanding in the learning of arithmetic procedures. *Cognition and Instruction, 8,* 103-179.

Opdenakker, M.-C., & Van Damme, J. (2006). Differences between secondary schools: A study about school context, group composition, school practice, and school effects with special attention to public and Catholic schools and types of schools. *School Effectiveness and School Improvement, 17,* 87-117.

Opdenakker, M.-C., Van Damme, J., De Fraine, B., Van Landeghem, G., & Onghena, P. (2002). The effects of schools and classes on mathematics achievement. *School Effectiveness and School Improvement, 13,* 399-427.

References   87

Padget, S. Y. (1998). Lessons from research on dyslexia: implications for a classification system for learning disabilities. *Learning Disability Quarterly, 21,* 167-178.

Pasnak, R., Cooke, W. D., & Hendricks, C. (2006). Enhancing academic performance by strengthening class-inclusion reasoning. *The Journal of Psychology, 140,* 603-613.

Passolunghi, M. C., Mammarella, I. C., & Altoe, G. (2008). Cognitive abilities as precursors of the early acquisition of mathematical skills during first through second grades. *Developmental Neuropsychology, 33,* 229-250.

Passolunghi, M.C., & Siegel, L.S. (2004). Working memory and access to numerical information in children with disability in mathematics. *Journal of Experimental Child Psychology, 88,* 348-367.

Piaget, J. (1965). *The child's conception of number.* New York: Norton.

Piaget, J. & Inhelder, B. (1959). *La genèse des structures logiques élémèntaires. Classification et sériation [The development of basic logical structures: Classification and seriation].* Neuchâtel France: Delachaux and Niestlé.

Piaget, J., & Szeminska, A. (1941). *La genèse du nombre chez l'enfant.* Neuchâtel: Delanchaux et Niestlé.

Piazza, M., Facoetti, A., Trussardi, A.N., Berteletti, I., Conte, S., Lucangeli, D., Dehaene, S., & Zorzi, M. (2010). Developmental trajectory of number acuity reveals a severe impairment in developmental dyscalculia, *Cognition, 115,* 10-25..

Porter, J. (1998). The understanding of counting in children with severe learning difficulties and nursery children. *British Journal of Educational Psychology, 68,* 331-345.

Reusser, K. (2000). Success and failure in school mathematics: effects of instruction and school environment. *European Child & Adolescent Psychiatry, 9,* II/7-II/26.

Rickard, T. C., Romero, S. G., Basso, G., Wharton, C., Flitman, S., & Grafman, J. (2000). The calculating brain: an fMRI study. *Neuropsycologia, 38,* 325-335.

Ricken, G., Fritz, A. (2006). Working memory functions in children with different arithmetical performance at kindergarten. *Psychologie in Erziehung und Unterricht, 53*, 263-274.

Rittle-Johnson, R., Siegler, R. S., & Wagner, M. (2001). Developing conceptual understanding and procedural skill in mathematics: An iterative process. *Journal of Educational Psychology, 93*, 346-362.

Robinson, C.S., Menchetti, B.M., Rogensen, J.K. (2002). Towards a Two-Factor Theory of One type of mathematics disability. Learning Disabilities: Research and Practice, 17, 81.

Rourke, B. P. (1989). *Nonverbal learning disabilities: The syndrome and the model.* New York: Guilford Press.

Rourke, B. P. (1993). Arithmetic disabilities, specific or otherwise: A neuropsychological perspective. *Journal of learning disabilities, 26,* 214-226.

Rourke, B. P. (Ed.). (1995). *Syndrome of nonverbal learning disabilities: Neurodevelopmental manifestations.* New York: Guilford Press.

Rourke, B. P., & Conway, J. A. (1997). Disabilities of arithmetic and mathematical reasoning: perspectives from neurology and neuropsychology. *Journal of learning disabilities, 30,* 34-46.

Rourke, B. P., & Finlayson, M. A. (1978). Neuropsychological significance of variations in patterns of academic performance : Verbal and visuo-spatial abilities. *Journal of Abnomral Child Psychology, 6,* 121-133.

Rourke, B. P., & Fuerst, D. R. (1995). Cognitive processing, academic achievement, and psychosocial functioning: A neuropsychological perspective. In. Cichetti, D. and Cohen, D. (Eds.), *Manual of developmental psychopathology* (Vol. 1, pp. 391-423). New York: Wiley.

Rouselle, L., & Noel, M.-P. (2007). Basic numerical skills in children with mathematics learning disabilities: A comparison of symbolic vs non-symbolic number magnitude processing. *Cognition, 102*, 361-395.

Ruijssenaars, A.J.J.M. (1992) *Rekenproblemen. Theorie, diagnostiek, behandeling [Arithmetic Difficulties: Theory, Assessment, Intervention].* Rotterdam: Lemniscaat.

References

89

Scruggs, T. E., & Mastropieri, M. A. (2002). On babies and bathwater: Addressing the problems of identification of learning disabilities. *Learning Disability Quarterly, 25,* 155-168.

Shalev, R. S. (2004). Developmental Dyscalculia. *Journal of Child Neurology, 10,* 766-771.

Shalev, R. S., Auerbach, J., Manor, O. and Gross-Tsur, V. (2000). Developmental dyscalculia: prevalence and prognosis. *European Child and Adolescent Psychiatry, 9,* II59-II64.

Shalev, R. S. & Gross-Tsur, V. (2001). Developmental dyscalculia. *Pediatric Neurology, 24,* 337-342.

Shalev, R., Manor, O., & Gros-Tsur, V. (2005). Developmental dyscalculia: A prospective six-year follow-up. *Developmental Medicine and Child Neurology, 47,* 121-125.

Shalev, R., Manor, O., Kerem, B., Ayali, M., Badichi, N., Friedlander, Y., & Gross-Tsur, V. (2001). Developmental dyscalculia is a familial learning disability. *Journal of Learning Disabilities, 34,* 59-65.

Sharon, T., & Wynn, K. (1998). Individuation of actions from continuous motion. *Psychological Science, 9,* 357-362.

Siegel, L. S. (1989). IQ is irrelevant to the definition of learning disabilities. *Journal of Learning Disabilities, 22,* 469-478.

Sophian, C. (1992). Learning about numbers: Lessons for mathematics education from preschool number development. In J. Bideaud, C. Meljac & J.-P. Fischer (Eds), *Pathways to number. Children's developing numerical abilities* (pp. 19-40). Hillsdale, NJ: Erlbaum.

Sophian, C., & Kailihiwa, C. (1998). Units of counting: developmental changes. *Cognitive Development, 13,* 561-585.

Sophian, C., Wood, A. M., & Vong, K. I. (1995). Making numbers count: the early development of numerical inferences. *Developmental Psychology, 31,* 263-273.

Spinath, B., Spinath, F. M., Harlaar, N., & Plomin, R. (2006). Predicting school achievement from general cognitive ability, self perceived ability, and intrinsic value. *Intelligence, 34,* 363-374.

Stanescu-Cosson, R., Pinel, P., Van De Moortele, P.F., Le Bihan, D., Cohen, L., & Dehaene, S. (2000). Understanding dissociations in dyscalulia. A brain imaging study of the impact of number size on the cerebral networks for exact and approximate calculation. *Brain, 123,* 2240-2255.

Starkey, P. (1992). The early development of numerical reasoning. *Cognition, 43,* 93-126.

Stock, P. (2008). *Prenumeric markers for arithmetic difficulties.* Unpublished doctoral research, Ghent University.

Stock, P., Desoete, A., & Roeyers, H. (2006). Focussing on mathematical disabilities: a search for definition, classisfication and assessment (pp. 29-62). In Soren V. Randall (Ed.) Learning Disabilities New Research *Nova Science: Hauppage, NY.*

Stock, P., Desoete, A., & Roeyers, H. (2007). Early markers for arithmetic difficulties. *Educational & Child Psychology, 24,* 28-39.

Stock, P., Desoete, A., & Roeyers, H. (2007). Dyscalculie, een stoornis met vele gezichten [Dyscalculia, a disability with many faces]. *Signaal, 59,* 22-42.

Stock, P., Desoete, A., & Roeyers, H. (2009a). Predicting Arithmetic Abilities: The Role of Preparatory Arithmetic Markers and Intelligence. *Journal of Psychoeducational Assessment,* 27, 237-251.

Stock, P., Desoete, A., & Roeyers, H. (2009b). Screening for mathematical disabilities in Kindergarten. *Developmental Neurohabilitation, 12,* 389-396.

Stock, P., Desoete, A., & Roeyers, H. (2009c). Mastery of the Counting Principles in Toddlers: A Crucial step in the Development of Budding Arithmetic Abilities? *Learning and Individual Differences, 19,* 419-422.

Stock, P., Desoete, A., & Roeyers, H. (2010). Detecting children with arithmetic disabilities from kindergarten: Evidence from a three year longitudional study on the role of preparatory arithmetic abilities. *Journal of Learning Disabilities, 43,* 250-268.

Strang, J. D., & Rourke, B. P. (1983). Concept-information / nonverbal reasoning abilities of children who exhibit specific academic problems with arithmetic. *Journal of Clinical Child Psychology, 12,* 33-39.

References 91

Temple, C.M. (1999). Procedural dyscalculia and number fact dyscalculia: Double dissociation in developmental dyscalculia. *Cognitive Neuropsychology, 8*, 155-176.

Torbeyns, J., Verschaffel, L., & Ghesquière, P. (2004). Strategic aspects of simple addition and subtraction: the influence of mathematical ability. *Learning and Instruction, 14*, 177-195.

Van Borsel, J. (1998). Rekenproblemen linguïstisch bekeken [A linguistic approach to arithmetic difficulties]. *Tijdschrift voor Logopedie en Audiologie, 28*, 6-11.

Van Harskamp, N. J., & Cipolotti, L. (2001). Selective impairments for addition, subtraction and multiplication. Implications for the organisationof arithmetical facts. *Cortex, 37*, 363-388.

Van De Rijt, B. A. M., & Van Luit, J. E. H. (1999). Milestones in the development of infant numeracy. *Scandinavian Journal of Psychology, 40*, 65-71.

Van De Rijt, B. A. M., Van Luit, J. E. H., & Pennings, A. H. (1996). Rekenvaardigheden van kleuters (1). Onderzoek in het basisonderwijs [Arithmetic abilities in toddlers (1). Research in elementary education]. *Tijdschrift voor Orthopedagogiek, 35*, 219-233.

Van der Sluis, S., de Jong, P. F., & van der Leij, A. (2007). Executive functioning in children, and its relations with reasoning, reading, and arithmetic. *Intelligence, 35*, 427-449.

Vanderswalmen, R., Vrijders, J., & Desoete, A. (2010). Metacognition and spelling performance in college students (pp. 367-394). In Efklides, A., & Misailidi, P. (Eds.). Trends and prospects in metacognition research. New York: Springer.

Van Luit, J. E. H. (2002). Rekenen bij jonge kinderen. In A. J. J. W. Ruijssenaars & P. Ghesquière (Ed.). *Dyslexie en dyscalculia: ernstige problemen in het leren lezen en rekenen. Recente ontwikkelingen in onderkenning en aanpak [Dyslexia and dyscalculia: serious problems in learning to read and to calculate. Recent developments in detection and remediation].* Acco: Leuven.

Van Steenbrugge, H., Valcke, M., & Desoete, A. (2010). Mathematics learning difficulties in primary education: teachers' professional knowledge and the use of commercially available learning packages. *Educational studies, 36,* 59-71.

von Aster, M. (2000). Developmental cognitive neuropsychology of number processing and calculation: varieties of developmental dyscalculia. *European Child and Adolescent Psychiatry, 9,* II/41-II/57.

von Aster, M. G., Deloche, G., Dellatolas, G. and Meier, M. (1997). Zahlenverarbeitung und Rechnen bei schulkindern der 2 und 3 Klassenstufe: Eine vergleichende Studie franzosischsprachiger und deutschsprachiger Kinder. *Zeitschift fur Entwicklungspsychologie und Padagogische Psychologie, 29,* 151-166.

Wilson, A., Revkin, S.K., Cohen, D., Cohen, L., & Dehaene, S. (2006). An open trial assessment for remediation of dyscalculia. *Behavioral and Brain Functions, 2*: 20.

World Health Organisation, 1992. *The ICD-10 Classification of mental and behavioural disorders. Clinical descriptions and diagnostic guidelines.* Geneva: WHO.

Wynn, K. (1990). Children's understanding of counting. *Cognition, 36,* 155-193.

Wynn, K. (1992). Children's acquisition of the number words and the counting system. *Cognitive Psychology, 24,* 220-251.

Wynn, K. (1996). Infants' individuation and enumeration of actions. *Psychological Science, 7,* 164-169.

Xu, F., & Arriaga, R.I. (2007). Number discrimination in 10-month-old infants. *British Journal of Developmental Psychology, 25,* 103-108.

Xu, F., & Spelke, E.S. (2000). Large number discrimination in 6-month-old infants. *Cognition, 74,* 1-11.

Xu, F., & Spelke, E.S., & Goddard, S. (2005). Number sense in human infants. *Developmental Science, 8,* 88-101.

INDEX

A

abstraction, 12, 13, 19
abstraction principle, 12, 13, 19
academic performance, 87, 88
academic problems, 90
achievement test, 42, 52
ADHD, 18
adolescents, 74, 76
aetiology, 3
American Psychiatric Association, 60, 73
American Psychological Association, 80
APA, 2, 3
arithmetic, vii, 1, 2, 3, 5, 7, 10, 11, 17, 24, 27, 33, 41, 46, 52, 76, 79, 80, 81, 82, 84, 85, 86, 88, 90, 91
assessment, 1, 6, 16, 18, 30, 42, 45, 57, 59, 60, 68, 69, 76, 78, 90, 92
assessment tools, 6
'at least moderate achieving' (MA), 18, 20, 21, 23, 24, 25, 81
automation, 10

B

behavioral problems, 18

brain, 18, 76, 87, 90
brain damage, 18

C

cardinality principle, 12, 13, 15, 30, 31, 32, 33, 50, 79
case study, 75
categorization, 59, 70, 84
Catholic school, 86
central executive, 65, 83
challenges, 16, 48, 66
childhood, iv, 39
classes, 41, 86
classification, 1, 2, 8, 14, 16, 19, 25, 26, 27, 37, 39, 43, 44, 45, 46, 47, 49, 51, 52, 54, 57, 58, 59, 62, 63, 64, 67, 68, 70, 76, 87
classroom, 31
cognition, 64, 79, 80, 81, 85
cognitive abilities, 62
cognitive ability, 89
cognitive antecedents, 7
cognitive development, 47, 79
cognitive process, 63, 65, 66
cognitive system, 66
college students, 91

Index

comparison task, 7, 16, 26, 45, 49, 50, 52, 56, 58, 64, 68, 70, 77
comprehension, 4, 8, 47
computation, 80
computational skills in grade 1, 8
computing, 11
consensus, 6, 77, 82
conservation, 8, 14, 16, 19, 25, 26, 27, 37, 38, 47, 49, 51, 54, 63
critical analysis, 83
criticism, 8, 55
cultural differences, 3
curriculum, 3

D

deficiencies, 59
deficit, 6, 7, 14, 45, 48, 64
dependent variable, 24, 31, 43, 50
detection, 6, 9, 14, 27, 39, 56, 60, 62, 69, 91
developmental change, 89
developmental disorder, 6
developmental process, 6
developmental psychopathology, 88
diagnostic criteria, 6
disability, 1, 2, 3, 5, 6, 18, 62, 68, 80, 81, 83, 85, 86, 87, 88, 89, 90
discriminant analysis, 20, 25, 43
discrimination, 75, 92
disorder, 3, 64, 73
dyslexia, 75, 87

E

economic status, 42
education, 86, 91, 92
educational background, 18, 51
elaboration, 4, 79
elementary school, 21, 42, 54, 64, 70, 76
environmental factors, 3
etiology, 83

evidence, 5, 11, 55, 56, 62, 65, 67, 68, 69, 70, 76
exclusion, 2, 3
executive function, 65

F

family members, 3
flexibility, 39
fluid intelligence, 36, 42
foundations, 13, 79

G

general intelligence, 3
gifted, 80
grades, 42, 52, 87
growth, 7, 11, 83
guidelines, 92

H

health, 18
history, 18
human, 92
hypothesis, 7, 9, 12, 31, 55, 57, 61, 69

I

identification, 62, 65, 68, 79, 82, 86, 89
impairments, 3, 48, 91
individual differences, 51, 82
individuation, 92
infancy, 75, 80
infants, 64, 75, 92
inferences, 89
initial mathematical performance, 7
integration, 56
intelligence, 6, 16, 36, 37, 38, 39, 43, 51, 62, 69, 83

Index

95

intervention, 9, 22, 66, 78, 79, 85, 86

intrinsic value, 89

K

kindergarten, iv, vii, 12, 14, 15, 16, 20, 21, 23, 26, 29, 30, 31, 32, 33, 35, 36, 38, 39, 41, 42, 43, 45, 46, 48, 49, 50, 51, 53, 54, 56, 57, 59, 61, 64, 68, 77, 83, 84, 88, 90

L

learning, 6, 7, 10, 13, 17, 18, 22, 29, 63, 73, 74, 76, 77, 78, 79, 80, 81, 82, 83, 85, 86, 87, 88, 89, 91, 92

learning difficulties, 22, 74, 87, 92

learning disabilities, 7, 17, 63, 73, 76, 77, 78, 79, 80, 82, 83, 85, 86, 87, 88, 89

learning process, 13, 76

logical abilities, vii, 7, 8, 9, 14, 15, 16, 24, 26, 47, 48, 49, 52, 54, 55, 57, 67, 71

logical reasoning, 86

longitudinal study, 14, 16, 41, 51, 52, 58, 62, 77, 80

'low achieving' (LA), 3, 15, 16, 18, 20, 21, 23, 24, 25, 26, 42, 43, 44, 45, 46, 49, 52, 53, 54, 55, 56, 58, 59, 60, 61, 62, 68, 69, 70, 78

M

magnetic resonance imaging, 74

magnitude, vii, 7, 13, 14, 15, 16, 24, 25, 26, 27, 43, 44, 45, 48, 49, 52, 56, 57, 58, 64, 65, 67, 68, 70, 76, 84, 88

magnitude processing deficit, 7

MANOVA, 24, 43

mathematical achievement, 31, 32, 33, 41, 44, 45, 48, 51, 52, 53, 59, 80

mathematical disabilities, iv, vii, 1, 2, 3, 4, 5, 6, 7, 10, 12, 13, 14, 15, 18, 20, 23, 39, 44, 45, 46, 47, 49, 52, 56, 57, 60, 61, 62, 64, 65, 66, 67, 68, 69, 70, 76, 77, 81, 90

mathematics, 3, 4, 7, 8, 9, 16, 17, 21, 25, 26, 33, 44, 45, 46, 48, 52, 53, 59, 60, 61, 76, 77, 78, 79, 80, 82, 83, 85, 86, 87, 88, 89

mathematics education, 77, 78, 89

mathematics tests, 33

measurement(s), 30, 63

memory, 4, 5, 9, 10, 65, 74, 83, 87, 88

memory function, 88

mental arithmetic, vii, 18, 33, 83

mental disorder, 2, 73

mental retardation, 3

metacognition, 65, 76, 78, 91

MLD, 85, 86

models, 4, 10, 56, 57, 64, 66, 67, 81

multiple regression, 20, 36, 37, 38

multiple regression analyses, 20

multiple regression analysis, 36, 37, 38

multiplication, 10, 74, 76, 91

multivariate analysis, 24, 43

N

native Dutch-speaking children, 18, 20, 29, 35, 41

neonates, 73

neuroimaging, 3

neuropsychology, 81, 88, 92

non-symbolic tasks, 7

non-symcolic (dot), 7

normal development, 10

O

one-one-correspondence principle, 12, 13, 30, 31, 32

operations, 9, 19, 24, 65, 74

order-irrelevance principle, 12, 13

organize, 81

P

parents, 18, 42
percentile, 2, 18, 23, 41, 52, 60
PET, 76
Piaget, 7, 8, 47, 54, 63, 85, 87
Piagetian abilities, 7
pilot study, vii, 15, 17, 21, 22, 49, 56, 57
preschool, 8, 11, 17, 18, 20, 21, 22, 89
preschoolers, 14
primary school, 85, 86
principles, 12, 13, 15, 16, 19, 22, 26, 30, 31, 32, 33, 50, 54, 55, 68, 81, 84
problem solving, 48, 67, 78, 79
procedural knowledge, 19, 22, 26, 36, 37, 55, 68, 84
prognosis, 83, 89
project, 54, 63, 65
psychosocial functioning, 88

R

reading, 61, 75, 79, 83, 84, 85, 86, 91
reading difficulties, 84
reading disability, 84
reasoning, 16, 18, 20, 21, 36, 37, 38, 39, 49, 50, 51, 57, 59, 62, 87, 88, 90, 91
reasoning skills, 21, 52
recommendations, iv
rehabilitation, 76
remediation, 62, 68, 69, 91, 92
researchers, 1, 4, 6, 9, 12, 13, 47, 48, 55, 64, 67, 70, 75, 77
retardation, 2, 16, 44
risk, 3, 15, 17, 20, 21, 22, 39, 45, 47, 49, 60, 62, 69, 70, 83
routes, 75

S

scholarship, 42
scholastic achievement, 51, 75
school, 1, 14, 29, 31, 33, 47, 51, 58, 59, 70, 83, 86, 87, 89
school achievement, 14, 47, 89
schooling, 7, 33, 47, 54, 65, 66, 70, 74
secondary schools, 86
semantic information, 64
semantic memory, 4, 5
sensory impairments, 3
SES, 42, 75
social support, 3
spelling, 91
stability, 83
stable order principle, 12, 13, 30, 32
subgroups, 83
subitizing, 7, 13, 63, 64
subtraction, 8, 10, 80, 91
symbolice, 7
symptoms, 48
syndrome, 85, 88

T

target, 20, 85
target number, 20
teachers, 21, 32, 33, 39, 70, 92
testing, 83
toddlers, 32, 91
training, 78, 84
training programs, 84
treatment, 2, 29, 62, 78

V

variables, 6, 14, 63, 67, 77
variations, 14, 64, 88
varieties, 82, 92

visual system, 65

W

Washington, 73, 80

Wechsler Intelligence Scale, 36, 42
working memory, 4, 9, 62, 65, 66
World Health Organisation (WHO), 2, 3, 92